JANE AUSTEN

JANE AUSTEN

by

B. C. SOUTHAM

Edited by Ian Scott-Kilvert

PUBLISHED FOR
THE BRITISH COUNCIL
BY LONGMAN GROUP LTD

LONGMAN GROUP LTD
Longman House, Burnt Mill, Harlow, Essex

*Associated companies, branches and
representatives throughout the world*

First published 1975
Reprinted with additions to the Bibliography 1976
© Brian Southam 1975

*Printed in England by
Bradleys, Reading and London*

ISBN 0 582 01243 0

Thanks are due to Faber & Faber Ltd, and to Random House Inc.,
New York, for permission to quote from *Letters from Iceland* by
W. H. Auden.

JANE AUSTEN

I

IT SEEMS a contradiction in terms to talk in the same breath about literary greatness and popularity. Almost by definition, a literary classic implies a minority audience, the professional attention of scholars and critics and the enforced attention of students. In this light, the case of Jane Austen is remarkable. This is a writer whose novels are among the acknowledged classics of English literature, studied in schools and universities throughout the world (at the latest count, in thirty-five languages, including Chinese, Japanese, Persian and Bengali), with an enormous bibliography of scholarship and criticism. Yet the six novels also attract an audience quite unconcerned about Jane Austen's critical reputation and status, who turn to the novels simply for enjoyment. This is the only instance in English literature where Dr Johnson's image of 'the common reader' really comes alive: the idea that the ultimate test of literary greatness is not in the formal recognition of the academics but rests with 'the common sense of readers, uncorrupted by literary prejudices'; and that this individual judgement should prevail over 'the refinements of subtlety and the dogmatism of learning'.

To stress Jane Austen's popularity is not to disparage the interest of critics and scholars. Literary historians delight in her ramified allusiveness. She is a critics' novelist *par excellence*, a writer whose subtlety and sophistication have always attracted subtle and sophisticated minds. The novels have proved to be wonderfully rewarding for interpretative critics who light on such a richness of meaning in their structure of language and the vibrations of irony. Rhetoricians of fiction have developed some of their finest discussions upon the study of her narrative methods. She is recognized as a supreme artist of the novel, a judgement that comes with special authority from other novelists as well as critics. The dramatic power of her characters led some nineteenth-century writers, including Macaulay and George Lewes, to regard her as no less than a 'prose Shakespeare'; and in our own day Brigid Brophy has described Jane Austen as 'the greatest novelist of all time'.

In these terms, Jane Austen's achievement sounds forbidding. But this is precisely what the novels are not. Whatever their dignity as works of literature, as books for reading their stance is completely unpretentious. They seem to offer themselves as no more than entertainment. Even after 160 years, they continue to provide what is for most people the prime satisfaction of reading—the chance to escape from the pressures of ordinary life into the security of a created world, where another order of reality takes over for a while. As Clerihew Bentley put it, 'The novels of Jane Austen / Are the ones to get lost in'. His doggerel captures a popular truth. Her picture of Regency England still exerts a containing and hypnotic realism. For all its selectivity and exclusions, its remoteness from us in time and culture, it is a fictional world into which the reader can move easily and within which there is a powerful illusion of completeness and truth. The distance in time is bridged by the momentum of the writing, its brilliance, stylishness and drive, by the fascination of the characters, by the skill of the story-telling and by the appeal of the author's sane and sympathetic humanity. The novels offer us the excitement of sharing the vision of a creative mind and of responding to its energies of wit and understanding. Many critics have devoted many books to the analysis of these effects. But in the end, we are left with the plain fact of Jane Austen's *readability* and within this her capacity to engage us imaginatively, emotionally and intellectually.

The publication of the six novels between 1811 and 1817 marked a turning-point in the development of English fiction. To Jane Austen's contemporary audience they revealed that the novel was capable of unsuspected power, that it was not to be dismissed as a mere pastime but was to be taken seriously as a form of literature, on a level with poetry and drama; and the early reviews by Scott and Richard Whately proved that criticism of the novel could itself rank as a serious intellectual activity. In the words of George Moore, Jane Austen turned the wash-tub into the vase. In effect, she transformed the eighteenth-century novel—which could be a clumsy and primitive performance, uncertain in its technique—into a work of art. She gave elegance and form to its shaping, style to its writing, and narrative skill to the presentation of the story. She invented her own special mode of fiction, the domestic comedy of middle-class manners, a dramatic, realistic account of the quiet backwaters of everyday life for the country families of Regency England from the late 1790s until 1815. Her account of this world is limited and highly selective. Its focus is upon the experiences of young women on the path to marriage; and there is no attempt to present a social panorama (as earlier novelists, such as Fielding and Smollett, had done), nor to describe the condition of industrial England and its appalling scenes of poverty and social unrest (a task which many Victorian novelists, from Dickens onwards, were to set themselves). The modesty of Jane Austen's fictional world is caught in her remark to a novel-writing niece that '3 or 4 Families in a Country Village is the very thing to work upon', and her famous comment to a novel-writing nephew about 'the little bit (two inches wide) of Ivory on which I work with so fine a Brush' which 'produces little effect after much labour'.

However, the claim to be a miniaturist is not to be taken at face value. There is certainly a miniaturism in the artistry of Jane Austen's language and the refinements of verbal style; and another kind of miniaturism in the tight social and geographical boundaries of the stories. But the novels themselves give an impression of size and strength; their fictional world is lucidly defined; they have dimensions of space and time and a firm logic of structure and organization. And within the limits of the 'Country Village' scene and its neighbourhood of respectable families, the novels communicate a profound sense of this moment in English history—when the old Georgian world of the eighteenth century was being carried uneasily and reluctantly into the new world of Regency England, the Augustan world into the Romantic. The detailed account of its manners and fashionable pursuits is the descriptive groundwork for a highly analytical portrait of the age, which in turn conveys an implication of the deeper processes of change in early nineteenth-century society and in the individual's understanding of himself and the world around him.

II

Historically, the novels are a challenge to the idea of society as a civilizing force and to the image of man's fulfilment as an enlightened social being. They question the driving optimism of the period—that this, in the development of English society, was triumphantly the Age of Improvement. Improvement was the leading spirit of Regency England, its self-awarded palm. Certainly it was unequalled as a period of economic improvement, in the wake of the industrial revolution. The wartime economy accelerated this new prosperity. Alongside this material improvement there was an air of self-conscious, self-congratulatory improvement in manners, in religious zeal, in morality, in the popularization of science, philosophy and the arts. It was the age of encyclo-paedias, displaying the scope and categories of human knowledge in a digestible form. Books and essays paraded 'Improvement' in their titles. In an essay 'On the means of improving the people' (meaning the working people), Southey struck a common chord of complacent Englander-ism, rejoicing to belong 'to the middle rank of life . . . which in this country and at this time [1818] is beyond doubt the most favourable situation wherein man has ever been placed for the cultivation of his moral and intellectual nature'.

But many of the achievements of Regency improvement were more apparent than real. This is nicely symbolized in its most conspicuous manifestation, across the countryside itself. Landscape improvement was celebrated as the latest of the fine arts, much theorized about by contemporary aestheticians and brandished as a distinctively English contribution to the sum of civilization. Country houses and their grounds were expensively and elaborately improved, as General Tilney's 'improving hand' has transformed the pre-Reformation convent of Northanger Abbey into a modern home of extravagant and faintly ludicrous luxury, and as in *Mansfield Park*, Repton, the fashionable improver of the day, is to transform Sotherton Court, a fine old Elizabethan country house, destined to be adorned in 'a modern dress'.

Throughout the novels Jane Austen plays deftly with the terminology of improvement, carrying its negative overtones of novelty, showiness and superficiality into the realm of manners, behaviour and morality. Improvement can be a façade, a veneer. Jane Austen's sceptical, testing irony is the acid solution to peel it off, exposing the ramshackle foundations of social and personal morality which improvement could flashily conceal. For Mr Rushworth, Sotherton is 'a prison—quite a dismal old prison', crying out for the hand of Repton, whose speciality was making old houses look 'cheerful'. But the improving hand that first gets to work is Henry Crawford's. The cheerfulness and freedom he brings to Sotherton's 'prison' is a sexual escapade with the owner's wife!

Socially and politically, improvement had a very bitter ring. Essentially, it was a middle-class conceit. Outside the gentry's world of property and privilege was a wholly different scene. Throughout this period, a third of the country, its labouring population, lived permanently on the verge of starvation, while the rich became even richer, their prosperity more blatant. In this fertile ground, revolutionary ideas took root; and the period from the beginning of the 1790s until the Peterloo Massacre of 1819 was the most violent and repressive time in English history since the Civil War. Habeas corpus was suspended. Freedom of speech and freedom of meeting were curtailed. Bread riots were met with force and with that blunt instrument the masses were kept down. Jane Austen gives no more than a fleeting glimpse of England's violence. In *Northanger Abbey*, the London mobs come in as a joke. We never see the grinding misery of the poor; they are simply objects of charity, to be visited with a bowl of soup. It was not that Jane Austen was unaware. Hampshire and Kent, where she spent most of her adult life, were as badly hit by agricultural poverty as any other part of England. She must have seen it for herself and read about it in the essays and pamphlets of crusading reformers; and met it poignantly in her favourite poet, Crabbe, who delivered a starkly unpastoralizing report of what he observed, 'the Village Life a Life of Pain'.

There is no answer to the charge that Jane Austen should have devoted her genius to portraying the condition of England in all its misery and horror; that indeed would have been the great heroic task for a Tolstoy, a Dickens, a Zola, a Steinbeck or a Lawrence; and she would never have succeeded. Writing out of the experiences that she knew intimately, and with the particular artistic gifts of ironic commentary and observation, she was able to do something else. The restricted social vision of the novels is a satire in itself. It presents a faithful image of the gentry's state of mind. Its limitations and exclusions are those of the prosperous, leisured middle-class consciousness—self-regarding and self-centred, with its trivial time-filling preoccupations. Its gaze was steadily averted from the unpleasant social realities of an economic system which enabled the gentry to enjoy this way of life. Their turning away from the visible truth was culpable. John Cartwright protested in 1812, 'English gentlemen are perpetually travelling. Some go to see lakes and mountains' (as Elizabeth Bennet travels north with the Gardiners on a tour of the Peak district); 'Were it not as allowable to travel for seeing the actual conditions of a starving people'.

One of Jane Austen's major achievements in the novels is to have captured the total illusion of the gentry's vision, the experience of living in privileged isolation, of being party to a privileged outlook, of belonging to a privileged community, whose distresses, such as they are, are private, mild and genteel. Each of the homes and neighbourhoods is its own 'little social commonwealth', a microcosm, the centre of a minute universe. The irony is implicit. The miniature issues of these little worlds, so realistic, so much the centre of the stage, vivid and magnified to the point of surrealism, imply another, larger world beyond: 'the flourishing grandeur of a Country, is but another term for the depression and misery of the people ... to speak of the expensive luxury and refinements of the age, is but, with cruel irony, to remind us how many myriads are destitute'. John Thelwall, in *The*

Peripatetic (1793), was presenting a line of argument which was familiar to Jane Austen's audience and which the novels artfully exploit. 'The depression and misery' of the common people was a theme she could never handle directly; her way was to treat it by silent implication.

But the silence is not total. Just once or twice there is an oblique glimpse of the macabre reality that lies outside the image of the gentry's mind. This happens, for example, when Jane Austen describes Lady Catherine de Bourgh's activities in the parish of Hunsford: 'whenever any of the cottagers were disposed to be quarrelsome, discontented or too poor, she sallied forth into the village to settle their differences, silence their complaints, and scold them into harmony and plenty'. The scolding is a black joke. Hunsford's 'poor' were people starving. Several chapters earlier in *Pride and Prejudice*, Catherine and Lydia Bennet bring home the latest military gossip: 'Much had been done, and much had been said in the regiment since the preceding Wednesday; several of the officers had dined lately with their uncle, a private had been flogged, and it had actually been hinted that Colonel Forster was going to be married'. The device here is incongruity (cf. Pope's 'Puffs, powders, patches, bibles, billets-doux'). The wit is literary but the joke is not. The 'private . . . flogged' was the recipient of lashes to the number of 750 or 1000. Such punishments were widely reported. When the book appeared in 1813, these facts were in the public mind. The British Army was then distinguished as the only European army outside Russia to retain flogging as a punishment. Its abolition was debated in Parliament in 1811 and 1812. In 1810, Cobbett had been charged with seditious libel and sentenced to two years' imprisonment for an anti-flogging article in the *Political Register*; Leigh Hunt got eighteen months for printing a similar article in *The Examiner*. Writing from prison, Cobbett continued his attack upon its hideous inhumanity and the nauseating hypocrisy of its official circumlocution, *corporal infliction*: 'Why not name the thing? *Flog is flog*'. Simply and laconically, Jane Austen did just that.

Flogging was one aspect of national repression. It was a punishment handed out to the militia, to wartime conscripts on duty in England, rather than to the regular troops serving in Europe. A similar reality of English life comes into chapter XIV of *Northanger Abbey*, where Henry Tilney makes fun of his sister for supposing that Catherine's mysterious hinting about 'something very shocking indeed' in London— 'uncommonly dreadful. I shall expect murder and every thing of the kind'—refers to a calamity that has actually happened. Catherine is merely talking about the latest Gothic novel; and Tilney enjoys himself, elaborating on his sister's fearful imaginings: 'she immediately pictured to herself a mob of three thousand men assembling in St George's Fields; the Bank attacked, the Tower threatened, the streets of London flowing with blood . . .'. His tone is mocking and light-hearted. How could anyone be so silly? But historically his sister's train of thought is completely credible. The novel is set at the turn of the century and in July 1795, there was a meeting of the radical London Correspondence Society, 100,000 strong, at St George's Fields. The speeches were inflammatory, with talk of 'the holy blood of Patriotism, streaming from the severing axe . . .'. In October, George III was jeered on his way to the state opening of Parliament, his carriage was pelted and a window cracked by a stone. The next day horse-guards and troops had to clear the mobs out of his way to the theatre. So Eleanor's misunderstanding and Tilney's joke touch upon circumstances bizarrely close to the truth. In this passage, Jane Austen raises the spectre of revolutionary uprising, a fear that haunted the establishment and the middle-classes throughout this period and found a terrible nemesis in the deaths of Peterloo.

Jane Austen uses Tilney again in this historical function in chapter XXIV, when he reproves Catherine for her Gothic imaginings about his father and his dead mother, the half-formed idea that General Tilney might have murdered her:

Dear Miss Morland, consider the dreadful nature of the suspicions you have entertained. What have you been judging from? Remember the country and the age in which we live. Remember that we are English, that we are Christians. Consult your own understanding, your own sense of the probable, your own observation of what is passing around you—Does our education prepare us for such atrocities? Do our laws connive at them? Could they be perpetrated without being known, in a country like this, where social and literary intercourse is on such a footing; where every man is surrounded by a neighbourhood of voluntary spies, and where roads and newspapers lay every thing open? Dearest Miss Morland, what ideas have you been admitting?

After this lecture, Catherine runs off 'with tears of shame'. Tilney is laying Gothic ghosts. But for the readers of *Northanger Abbey*, in 1818, the joke is hollow; the passage rings with a disquieting truth and his reference to 'a neighbourhood of voluntary spies' is a figure of speech unpleasantly literal. 'Spies' were paid informers. At this time there was an extensive 'Spy-System' (as it was then known), maintained by the government to infiltrate working-men's organizations. Informing was promoted as a citizen's patriotic duty. In Parliamentary debates in the summer of 1817, the Prime Minister, Castlereagh, maintained that 'morality, religion, and social order, are best defended at home by spies and informers'. But the spy-system was vigorously challenged then, as it had been years before, in the early 1790s, when it was employed to counter the earliest radical groups. While there was deep fear that the horrors of the French Revolution would be enacted here, nonetheless the incursions of state repression were strongly opposed. In 1812, one critic went so far as to describe the police as 'a system of tyranny; an organized army of spies and informers, for the destruction of all public liberty, and the disturbance of all private happiness'. This was a Gothicism of Regency life, all too real, that Tilney's well-bred and enlightened reasonableness could never rob of its terrors.

It is with such momentary and glancing allusions that Jane Austen reminds the reader of the England unseen, that lies beyond the blinkered social focus of the gentry's vision. But these are pin-points of light. There was another 'depression and misery' that she knew intimately, and could command fully and creatively. This was the private, personal history of women like herself, trapped and stifled within the confines of a hot-house society, recognizing its brittleness and artificiality, but with no other world to exist in. These historical issues bear most immediately upon Jane Austen as a *woman* novelist, presenting an account of society from the woman's point of view—the woman's experience of men, of other women, of their families, the social circles to which they were confined, and, ultimately their experience of themselves and of life. For the first time in English literature, outside Shakespeare, we meet heroines who are credible, with minds, with the capacity to think for themselves, with ambition and wit, with an interior life independent of men and the will to challenge them emotionally and intellectually, with the energy to shape their relationships. The intense inner drama of the novels arises from the conflict between the individuality of the heroines, their private needs and aspirations, and the levelling, restrictive pressures of a tight social morality. Their predicament is to be born into a world which values them for their marriageability, where the culmination of womanhood is to be a wife and mother, where their lives are regulated by the artificial ideals of polite femininity. The six novels are repeated dramatizations of this theme. Each of the heroines has to learn to understand herself and her relationships with other people. She has to practise the morality of compromise and discover her own way of accepting the demands of society while preserving the integrity of her own values and beliefs. Each of the heroines travels the path of self-discovery and growth; they struggle towards self-determination and fulfilment; and Jane Austen leaves it an open question, open to us as readers to decide, how far they win through, how far they fail.

The recognition of this theme shows us how inadequate it is to label Jane Austen as a 'woman' writer or as 'the novelist of Regency England'. These labels are accurate and they draw attention to important aspects of her work. But her theme has as much to do with men as with women and it relates to any society which imposes a strict code of manners and tightly-defined roles upon the people who exist within it. Jane Austen's attitude may seem unheroic. She has no stirring message, no doctrine of personal liberation. Her view is coldly realistic. She presents the sad truth that however much people may dream of personal freedom, of escaping from the constrictions of their family or of society at large, we are nonetheless tied by blood and time and circumstance with bonds of need and dependence, to people we hate or despise or are bored by, yet cannot do without. Man's inhumanity to man can be polite, intimate and domestic. The novels confirm that life is a comedy to those who think. A thinking novelist, she casts her heroines in a thinking mould. But this single truth is not exclusive: life is also a tragedy to those who feel. And the deepest and most powerful tension arises from Jane Austen's struggle to maintain a hold over experiences that threaten the comic surface of the novels with the 'feeling' tones of tragedy.

III

Some books leave us totally incurious about their authors. In the novels of Jane Austen, however, the writer's presence is strongly marked, not just in an official role, as narrator or commentator, but as an active, pervasive 'artistic' presence—controlling, arranging, manipulating—reminding us continually that the realism of the novels is wholly artificial, wholly an effect of technique; not 'realism' created out of the vast, detailed sprawl of 'naturalism', but an economic, succinct realism formed out of the selection of detail and the synergy of its relationships. The realism is moral as well as aesthetic; it offers an interpretation and criticism of life, as well as a picture of it; and unless the reader deliberately switches off, its assertion of values leaves no room for indifference, and a great deal of room for reservation and disagreement.

Many readers respond to the novels at an extremely personal level, finding a 'Gentle Jane', a presence that is intimate and lovable. Katherine Mansfield declared that 'every true admirer of the novels cherishes the happy thought that he alone—reading between the lines—has become the secret friend of their author'. These are sentimental delusions but proudly confessed to. A. C. Bradley, the great Shakespearian critic, spoke of Elizabeth Bennet as a girl we are meant to fall in love with, as he did. Kipling wrote two poems in Jane Austen's honour, one of which ends with the stirring cry, 'Glory, love, and honour unto England's Jane'. The other, entitled 'Jane's Marriage', has her transported to Paradise. When she asks for 'Love', Captain Wentworth is called up from 'a private limbo', where he has been reading a copy of *Persuasion*, which 'told the plain / Story of love between / Him and Jane'. These two poems frame a story called 'The Janeites'. This is narrated by a soldier in the trenches in the First World War. In full, fruity cockneyese, he holds forth on his discovery that the ladies and gentlemen of the novels 'was only just like people you run across any day' and connects them incongruously with figures in his own life. He has learnt about Jane Austen from his officers, the Janeites of the title, who form their own little secret society, with its code of knowing catch-words and allusions to the novels. The fiction is answered in fact, for the Janeites still exist, enthusiasts who know the novels through and through, read and re-read them, see her characters in the world around them, and talk and write about Jane Austen with an amazing intimacy and affection. Some critics dismiss the Janeite following as cultish and sentimental. This may or may not be so. What is indisputable is the depth of the Janeite response to a quality of the author's personality that comes across with a living force.

But other readers find this personality unsympathetic, even repellent. Charlotte Brontë discovered a writer altogether out of touch with the 'Passions', 'a complete and most sensible lady, but a very incomplete, and rather insensible (*not senseless*) woman'. Mark Twain boasted that she awakened in him nothing less than an 'animal repugnance'. D. H. Lawrence admired the vivid presentation of her characters, but he abhorred the writer, 'a narrow-gutted spinster'. He enlarged upon this remark in 'A Propos of *Lady Chatterley's Lover*', where he mourned the loss of what he calls the 'blood-connexion' that linked the classes in the England of Defoe and Fielding: 'And then, in the mean Jane Austen, it is gone. Already this old maid typifies "personality" instead of character, the sharp knowing of apartness instead of knowing in togetherness, and she is, to my feeling, thoroughly unpleasant, English in the bad, snobbish sense of the word, just as Fielding is English in the good, generous sense'.

These comments have a historical force as well as a personal validity. Charlotte Brontë is voicing a mid-nineteenth-century Romantic position, objecting to Jane Austen's morality of self-discipline, good sense and rational feeling, and classifying her as a 'society' novelist, not a novelist of humanity. Lawrence invokes a twentieth-century psychological romanticism, arbitrary but illuminating. During the later eighteenth century, English society lost the last vestiges of social unity, its paternalistic 'blood connexion', the better side of feudalism. By Jane Austen's day this had given way to a divisive class-system with its elaborate snobberies of money and rank. To this extent, the 'knowing of apartness' that Lawrence identified in the novels is an authentic social experience, not solely a projection of some psychological apartness in Jane Austen's own make-up.

Jane Austen's spinsterdom is also taken up in W. H. Auden's verse-epistle, 'Letter to Lord Byron', in which he asks the poet to tell her 'How much her novels are beloved down here' and continues with a confession of his own discomfort at finding such a streak of cold realism in her nature:

> You could not shock her more than she shocks me:
> Beside her Joyce seems innocent as grass.
> It makes me most uncomfortable to see
> An English spinster of the middle class
> Describe the amorous effects of 'brass',
> Reveal so frankly and with such sobriety
> The economic basis of society.

Auden's point is that Jane Austen behaves out of character—fancy an English lady, a spinster at that, betraying the secrets of her class! Auden's 'shock' is a silent allusion to the popular myth of 'Gentle Jane'—an eternal Maiden Aunt, an inspired amateur in the best English tradition, the homely spinster who put down her stitching to pick up her pen, who wrote in odd moments snatched from her domestic round, a kind of Sunday writer, who scribbled just to please herself and entertain the family, who sat quietly in the corner, silently observing the world go by, catching a turn of phrase, the flow of conversation, sketching the characters and mannerisms of her neighbours and friends, describing their comings and goings, their contretemps, their joys and sadnesses, their follies, stupidities and mentionable vices. This notion of Jane Austen's unpretentious amateurism is a touching picture with some fragments of truth. The novels were indeed based upon direct observation; and we can see from her letters that the world of the fiction is a faithful account of the small social world in which she passed her days—with its local balls, its gossip, chatter and scandalizing, its marriageable young ladies and eligible young men.

But there the myth dissolves. The facts of Jane Austen's life tell a different story, one which confirms everything that the novels convey of their author's professionalism, her capacity for critical, creative detachment and her total artistic command over the daily experiences by which her writing was fed. The sheer readability of the novels seems so natural and effortless that we take it for granted, just as we accept the feat of realism and the vitality of the characters. As Virginia Woolf recognized, 'Of all great writers she is the most difficult to catch in the act of greatness'. How difficult, and deceptive, we can see in the remarks of Henry James, who identified the 'little touches of human truth, little glimpses of steady vision, little master-strokes of imagination', but put them down to 'the extraordinary grace of her facility . . . of her unconsciousness'. He was deceived by the art that conceals art. Seeing no evidence of effort, he supposed there was none, unaware that the achievement of the novels was the fruit of twenty years' apprenticeship, of a style and technique evolved through constant experiment, and that the story of her life is not just that of a writer, but of a writer determined to be published, determined to find an audience beyond the admiring circle of her family and friends, and determined to formulate a mode of social satire that would enable her to practise as a critic from within, delighting her audience with a portrait of themselves, flattering and entertaining in its mimetic accuracy but scathing in its judgement and in the implication of its silent exclusions. G. K. Chesterton observed that 'Jane Austen may have been protected from truth: but it was precious little of truth that was protected from her'. The novels wear a deceptive charm; as Richard Simpson explained it, 'a magnetic attractiveness which charms while it compels'; and their air of modesty is the modesty of Swift's *A Modest Proposal*, insidious and explosive.

IV

Jane Austen's life was private and uneventful; and by modern standards extraordinarily narrow and restricted. Her forty-two years, from 1775 to 1817, were passed entirely among her family and friends. She visited London from time to time but never mixed in fashionable society and avoided literary circles like the plague. 'If I am a wild beast, I cannot help it'. She never married; she never travelled abroad; she was unknown to the public. The novels were published anonymously and her authorship was revealed only after her death, through a biographical notice that came out with *Northanger Abbey* and *Persuasion* at the end of 1817. The pattern of her life was set by her dedication to writing and this in turn may help us to understand her obsessive need for privacy, her choice of spinsterdom and her role in the family as a dutiful daughter, an affectionate sister and a favourite aunt to hordes of nephews and nieces. The circumstances of her life also help us to understand certain qualities in her writing—its highly personal tone; its allusiveness; its dramatic aspect, in the prominence of dialogue and in the scene-like staging of the characters and action; and its concentration on personal and family relationships.

Her childhood was spent in the small Hampshire village of Steventon, where her father, George Austen, was the parish clergyman. It was a large and literary household. Her father was a classical scholar with a taste for fiction, including the Gothic thrillers that Jane Austen was to make fun of in *Northanger Abbey*. Her mother was well known for her impromptu poems and stories. Whilst at Oxford, her brothers Henry and James edited a literary periodical, *The Loiterer*, between 1789 and 1790. There was a tradition of reading aloud; and with two daughters and five sons, the family was able to put on plays. Friends and relatives were recruited and the rectory barn was converted into a small theatre for summer performances, while during the winter they played in the rectory itself. Among the productions were farces whose humour could be very broad and un-rectorylike.

From the outset, Jane Austen enjoyed the encouragement of a close and appreciative audience. Her early writing, dating from about 1787, the so-called *Juvenilia*, has come down to us in three manuscript notebooks, which contain pieces going up to about 1793. Soon after that, she wrote her first important work, a novel-in-letters, entitled *Lady Susan*. About 1795, she began another epistolary novel, 'Elinor and Marianne', which was eventually turned into *Sense and Sensibility*. In 1796–97, she completed the earliest version of *Pride and Prejudice*, then called 'First Impressions', which her father tried unsuccessfully to get published. In the next year, *Northanger Abbey* was written.

Until this time, Steventon had provided an ideal context for her work. The family was a keen audience. There was a wide neighbourhood of visitable families, of clergymen and local gentry; and further afield, throughout Southern England, the West Country and the Midlands, there was an extensive network of Austens and Leighs (her mother's family) to be visited. But this pattern of life changed in 1801 when Mr Austen gave up his parish and retired to Bath with his wife, Jane and Cassandra. He died in 1805 and, until 1809, they had to put up with a succession of temporary lodgings, or long visits to their relatives, in Bath, London, Clifton, Stoneleigh Abbey, Warwickshire (the family-seat of the Leighs) and Southampton. During this period, Jane Austen wrote little. The moves upset her; and there were other disappointments. In 1803, the manuscript of *Northanger Abbey* had been sold to a publisher, but was never printed. In December 1804, she lost her closest friend, Anne Lefroy, and a month later her father died. These events seem to have stopped her work on *The Watsons*, a manuscript she abandoned altogether. Its social picture is one of unrelieved bleakness, its heroine distressed, and its satire sharp to the point of cruelty. It signals a failing of generosity, a loss of creative power, which may stem from the sadness of these years.

In 1809 Jane Austen came to her last home, Chawton

Cottage, two miles south of Alton on the Winchester road, and not far from Steventon. Here she spent the remaining years of her life. The return to a settled domestic existence seems to have revived her energies. She took up the manuscripts of *Sense and Sensibility* and *Pride and Prejudice* to get them ready for publication; and in 1811 a publisher agreed to produce the first of these novels with her guarantee against loss. In 1811 she also began *Mansfield Park*, which was completed in the summer of 1813 and published in 1814. Between January 1814 and March 1815 she wrote *Emma*, which appeared at the end of 1815. *Persuasion* was written between August 1815 and August 1816; and in 1816 she also revised *Northanger Abbey*.

In January 1817, she began *Sanditon*, her seventh novel, writing and revising more than 24,000 words in eight weeks. But by then she was far into her last illness and the manuscript was put aside. It is an amazing document, a fierce and energetic satire on invalidism and hypochondria, Jane Austen's wry protest at her own condition. In May she was taken to Winchester to be under the care of a surgeon. Her illness was then unidentified; we now know it to have been Addison's disease. On the morning of July 18, at 4.30 a.m., she died. Asked for her last wishes, she replied, with characteristic dignity, economy and wit, 'I want nothing but death'. Six days later she was buried in Winchester Cathedral.

The course of Jane Austen's emotional life is obscure. The earliest of her surviving letters date from 1796 when she was twenty-one. They tell us of the parties and dances she went to locally, about visits to London, Bath and to the coast. But there is virtually nothing about her relationships with men. The few comments are ironic and evasive. All we have are some tantalizing stories in the family recollections and memoirs: that there was a mild flirtation with a young Irishman in 1796; that two or three years later she may have turned down a Fellow of Emmanuel College, Cambridge, staying in the locality; that in November 1802 she agreed to marry a Hampshire man, but that she changed her mind the very next morning. There are a number of other stories connecting her with someone—a naval officer, an army officer, or a clergyman—with whom she is said to have fallen in love but who died before their friendship could develop. There is no way of enlarging upon these vague and contradictory reports, for Cassandra destroyed her sister's most intimate letters. What remains, in the novels themselves, in *Sense and Sensibility* and *Persuasion* most of all, is the unquestionable proof that their author profoundly understood the experience of love, of love broken and disappointed, and the pains of loss and loneliness. As the Victorian novelist Julia Kavanagh observed, 'If we look under the shrewdness and quiet satire of her stories, we shall find a much keener sense of disappointment than of joy fulfilled. Sometimes we find more than disappointment.'

It seems unlikely that we shall ever know why Jane Austen remained unmarried. There may be a faint clue in *Lady Susan*. The heroine is a woman with a dominant, aggressive personality, talents which lead her to the brink of social self-destruction. It is a study in frustration, of a woman's fate when society has no use for her stronger, more 'masculine' talents. How far are we entitled to read this as a self-admonitory fable? Certainly, Jane Austen at seventeen was already in command of a powerful intellect which was to be turned more and more searchingly upon the people around her. Later in life she was described as 'a poker of whom everyone is afraid'. The remark is malicious. But it conveys an element of truth. Jane Austen must have been a formidable woman to meet, even as a young woman. In Kipling's sympathetic fantasy-poem, Jane Austen is a sadly resigned Anne Elliot who missed her Wentworth. This image of the older woman needs to be balanced with an image of Jane Austen when young—an Elizabeth Bennet, brilliant, vivacious and witty, yet critical, challenging and demanding, a woman who asked something of life and who never met a Darcy who could match her.

V

The six novels fall into two distinct groups. The early novels —*Sense and Sensibility*, *Pride and Prejudice* and *Northanger*

Abbey—were begun in the 1790s, and were rewritten and revised before their eventual publication; whereas the three later novels—*Mansfield Park*, *Emma* and *Persuasion*—belong entirely to Jane Austen's years of maturity. This order helps us to trace Jane Austen's technical development in the art of narration and to follow the changes in her view of life. Qualities in the early novels seem to mark them as the work of a younger woman while the imaginative temper of the second group is different. There is also the question of historical change. Jane Austen was thinking of this when she revised *Northanger Abbey* in 1816. She provided an 'Advertisement' warning readers that the book had originally been intended for publication in 1803, 'that thirteen years have passed since it was finished, many more since it was begun, and that during that period, places, manners, books, and opinions have undergone considerable changes'. This warning was more necessary than Jane Austen could have guessed, for the publication of *Northanger Abbey* was delayed until the end of 1817, when it came out as part of a four-volume set alongside *Persuasion*. Both novels have a Bath setting. But a great deal had happened to society during these years. While the story of *Northanger Abbey* is undated, its fashions and literary jokes belong firmly to the turn of the century. In *Persuasion*, the story is precisely dated and the sequence of contemporary events is used to work the story's plot: its beginning in 'the summer of 1814' is a prelude to Wentworth's return from duty at sea; in April 1814, Napoleon abdicated; and in the autumn, released from active service, Wentworth comes back on leave to Somerset. Eight years before, as a penniless Lieutenant, with a chancy life at sea, he was not considered a fit match for a Baronet's daughter. But now the situation has changed. He is a Captain, with a modest fortune in prize-money. Although the Wentworths are nobodies alongside the ancient lineage of the Elliots, he has been made socially respectable by the new heroic dignity of his profession. The nation was indebted to its navy, both for the victories at sea and the safeguarding of Britain's trading routes.

The historical distance between *Northanger Abbey* and *Persuasion* also brings out another major feature of Jane

Austen's development, the gradual shift of emphasis from literary to social satire. Her earliest creative impulse, as we can see it in the *Juvenilia*, was distinctively *critical*. The childhood pieces parody virtually every style of fiction around her in the 1790s, and the three early novels develop directly out of that tradition. Although none of the manuscripts survive, we can reconstruct the process by which they were transformed from straight parody into realistic comedy-of-manners. *Northanger Abbey* looks as if it was put together from two separate pieces: a skit on the Fanny Burney style of social novel, telling of a young woman's first experience of polite society; added to a satire on Gothic fiction. *Sense and Sensibility* began as a novel-in-letters, mocking Marianne Dashwood as a heroine of sensibility, from sentimental fiction, and exposing her correspondence to the comments of her sensible sister Elinor, who would give her sound advice on controlling her feelings, in the style of conduct fiction. 'First Impressions', the original version of *Pride and Prejudice*, takes its title directly out of the terminology of sentimental fiction, where it meant trust in one's immediate feelings, usually love at first sight.

In rewriting these early versions, it was not Jane Austen's purpose to remove the literary satire altogether, but to adjust it to a more realistic social setting. The final *Northanger Abbey* remains a Gothic satire; Marianne Dashwood still carries traces of her literary origin, and occasionally shifts back into her former role as a joke-heroine; and the 'First Impressions' theme is carried strongly into *Pride and Prejudice*. Neither did Jane Austen's interest in literary satire peter out. It was an experience that she shared with her readers and it continued, at a more subdued level throughout the later novels, until *Sanditon*, where, strangely, literary satire comes to the fore again. Today, this may seem to be a rather specialized matter. But for Jane Austen and her contemporaries, literature carried an important social and cultural significance and the novel in particular played a vital part in creating an image of middle-class identity; indeed, the novel was a product of middle-class society, catering to its interests and tastes.

Its rise, in England, came in the eighteenth century with the growth of an increasingly prosperous and leisured reading public. With the new wealth of the industrial revolution, this audience grew rapidly. By the 1770s novel-writing had become a largely commercial activity and literary hacks produced a flood of popular reading, the 'mere trash of the circulating library', as Jane Austen described it. The character of this fiction was determined largely by the character of its public, an audience of women with time and money on their hands and an appetite for easy reading. There was still an audience for the picaresque stories of Defoe, Fielding and Smollett, with their coarse vitality and the knock-about humour of low life. But the fashionable female audience ('our fair readers' to the writers and reviewers) wanted a literature flattering to them, that celebrated the arrival in English life of an improved level of society, and in which women were seen to have the good taste to cultivate their finer feelings and to develop an elaborate code of manners.

There developed a bewildering variety of fictional types and sub-types. But one principle runs throughout the 'society' literature of this period—the cult of feeling. This is one aspect of the eighteenth-century shift from the Age of Reason to Romanticism; and its significance as a symptom of deeper cultural change should not be ignored. But in fiction it had a very degraded 'social' manifestation for readers who practised a snobbery of feeling to differentiate themselves from previous generations. Sensibility became the class badge of polite society; and the central figure of its literature was the so-called sentimental heroine of feeling. Her heroism is measured by the strength of her passions and the delicacy with which her sensibility trembles. Heroines prove their ladylikeness in displays of feeling, in blushes, tears, hysterics, swoonings and madness. Lovers fall in love at sight; they are wracked by passion and the pangs of separation; and are elevated by the portrayable ecstasies of union. The plots were designed to throw them into a succession of dangers, both moral and physical, from which they could be rescued by heroes of exemplary courage and virtue. In Gothic versions, they would be swept away, in distant times, to the remote medieval gloom of crumbling fortresses ruled over by Germanic or Italianate Barons.

The cult of sensibility runs throughout the fiction of this period, in historical romances (where there was often a quieter responsiveness to the charms of the past or to an evocative, melancholic landscape), even in the novels of Fanny Burney, the only writer at this time to make a genuine attempt to portray the realities of life for a young woman entering polite society. Jane Austen was not the only one to react critically. Moralists attacked the cult as a dangerous, deceptive poisoner of impressionable young minds, while satirists made fun of it.

Northanger Abbey itself stands in a flourishing tradition of the mock-Gothic. However, Jane Austen was alone in understanding the potentialities of fiction as a form of literature, a belief that she doesn't force upon her readers, but which she tried to realize in her own writing, and to which she alluded jokingly in chapter V, where she reports a typical 1790s conversation:

'I am no novel reader—I seldom look into novels—Do not imagine that I often read novels—It is really very well for a novel.' —Such is the common cant.—'And what are you reading, Miss-?' 'Oh! it is only a novel' replies the young lady; while she lays down her book with affected indifference, or momentary shame.—'It is only Cecilia, or Camilla, or Belinda;' or, in short, only some work in which the greatest powers of the mind are displayed, in which the most thorough knowledge of human nature, the happiest delineation of its varieties, the liveliest effusions of wit and humour are conveyed to the world in the best chosen language.

The rhetorical claim of the last five lines is an irony in itself. This is exactly what the contemporary novel was *not*, not even the works of Fanny Burney named here; and Jane Austen is able to say this because she knew so clearly what had once been achieved half a century before in the hands of Fielding and Richardson, and what could be achieved again, through her own work.

In Catherine Morland, Jane Austen presents a stock figure of current satire, the young woman so captivated by the exotic thrills of the Gothic that she is ready to see the world through the lens of her latest reading, in this case the most popular of all such novels, *The Mysteries of Udolpho* (1794) by Mrs Radcliffe. Employing this common satirical device, Jane Austen's special twist was to show that the heroine doesn't have to look for excitement in books since there is a Gothicism of ordinary life, which can be experienced in the clear light of day.

This is the literary beginning to an issue raised again and again for the heroines of the six novels—the need to distinguish between illusion and reality, to be aware that the imagination has the power to enforce its own slanted vision upon the world. It is part of the struggle that the heroines have with the forces of pride and prejudice and with sense and sensibility, and which Emma Woodhouse faces in romantically casting Harriet Smith in the role of a distressed heroine and herself as a confidante-saviour. The educative process of the novels is to take the heroines along the path of disillusionment towards a clearer, unimpeded knowledge of themselves and their relationships, and the literary delusion is one of the blocks that they have to overcome.

Jane Austen's anti-romanticism was identified by Sir Walter Scott in 1816 in his review of *Emma*. He remarked that the story has 'cross purposes enough (were the novel of a more romantic cast) for cutting half the men's throats and breaking half the women's hearts'. No throats are cut; no hearts are broken. The novel plays with the devices and situations of romantic fiction, adjusting them to a story whose dramas and distresses are personal and domestic. Scott was looking at *Sense and Sensibility* and *Pride and Prejudice* as well; and he used this review as an occasion for placing Jane Austen's achievement in a new realist tradition of contemporary life. Whereas the sentimental romance purported to be an imitation of *la belle nature*, a higher and a nobler reality, to be aspired to, Jane Austen provided its antithesis, an imitation of the tempo and character of ordinary existence, to be faced, as Elizabeth Elliot in *Persuasion* faces 'the sameness and the elegance, the prosperity and the nothingness of her scene of life . . . a long uneventful residence in one country circle'. In the works of Jane Austen, Scott declares, we have the accuracy and realism of 'the modern novel'.

We can extend this historical placing by a glance sideways

to the situation in poetry at this time. Jane Austen's critical response to fiction is almost exactly matched in Wordsworth's critical reaction to the state of verse. Like her, he found himself surrounded by a tired, imitative school of writing, highly conventionalized and remote from the language and lives of ordinary people. His creative counter-statement was the poetry of the *Lyrical Ballads* (1798); and his formal protest was the 'Advertisement' to that volume and the 'Preface' to the second edition (1800), where he complained, in words that Jane Austen could very well have used herself, of the public appetite for melodrama and extravagance, 'this degrading thirst after outrageous stimulation' and the 'frantic novels' which were currently so popular. He drew attention to his choice of 'incidents and situations from common life', presented, as far as possible, in 'a selection of language really used by men', a formula which applies, with only a modification upwards into middle-class life, to Jane Austen's procedure in the novels. Just as the *Lyrical Ballads* set a standard in poetry, so her writing provided an implicit commentary on the state of English fiction as she found it in the 1790s. Her work was in effect a liberation of the novel from its servile function as a class-entertainment and as an instrument of cultural self-flattery. She showed instead that fiction could present an artistic image, delightful for its accuracy and realism, yet disturbing too, for within this accuracy and realism lay the incisive, anatomizing, analytical truth of its commentary upon middle-class life and manners.

VI

Jane Austen's contemporary readers paid her the highest possible tribute to an artist in the realist tradition—they confused her fiction with reality. She was plagued by people who went round finding originals for the characters. In June 1814, a month after the publication of *Mansfield Park*, she met a fantasticating Miss Dusautoy, who had 'a great idea of being Fanny Price—she and her youngest sister together, who is named Fanny'. Then there was the deluded Miss

Isabella Herries who having read *Emma* was 'convinced that I had meant Mrs & Miss Bates for some acquaintance of theirs—People whom I never heard of before'. We can smile at their *naïveté* and share Jane Austen's annoyance that strangers should foist such silly identifications upon her (including the suggestion that the Dashwood sisters in *Sense and Sensibility* were portraits of herself and her sister Cassandra). But, in all their simplicity, these comments testify to the convincing dramatic life of her characters. This quality was more deeply experienced by a Mrs Cage who came away from *Emma*, her imagination bemused: 'I am at Highbury all day', she reported, 'and I can't help feeling I have just got into a new set of acquaintances'. A cooler, more analytical note is struck by Lady Harriet Gordon, who read *Mansfield Park* when it first appeared and whose comments Jane Austen considered important enough to place in a collection of 'Opinions':

In most novels you are amused for the time with a set of Ideal People whom you never think of afterwards or whom you the least expect to meet in common life, whereas in Miss Austen's works, and especially in Mansfield Park you actually *live* with them, you fancy yourself one of the family; and the scenes are so exactly descriptive, so perfectly natural, that there is scarcely an incident or conversation, or a person that you are not inclined to imagine you have at one time or other in your Life been a witness to, born a part in, and been acquainted with.

The same point was developed more systematically by contemporary reviewers. An anonymous contributor to the *British Critic* for March 1818 remarked that 'we instantly recognize among some of our acquaintances, the sort of persons she intends to signify, as accurately as if we had heard their voices'; 'she seems to be describing such people as meet together every night in every respectable house in London; and to relate such incidents as have probably happened one time or other, to half the families in the United Kingdom'. One of the characters picked out is Isabella Thorpe from *Northanger Abbey*, 'a fine handsome girl, thinking of nothing but finery and flirting, and an exact representation of that large class of young women in the form they assume among the gayer part of the middling ranks of society'. Like other reviewers, he was struck by the accuracy as well as the lifelikeness of Jane Austen's social portraiture; her characters are seen to be representative types; and in these comments we can gauge the immediate success of the novels in the comedy of manners tradition.

In English fiction, we are familiar with the comedy of manners through the works of Thackeray, Trollope, George Eliot, E. M. Forster, and in more recent novelists, including Evelyn Waugh and Antony Powell. But in Jane Austen's day, it was essentially a dramatic tradition, beginning in the Restoration theatre and revived in the later eighteenth century by Garrick and Sheridan. It was a tradition in which Jane Austen was well-grounded. The Steventon productions had included plays by Sheridan and Garrick, as well as by a number of minor dramatists of the time; and as a girl she had experimented with scenes of burlesque drama. This theatrical tradition was a potent force in shaping Jane Austen's method in the novels, where so much of the action is realized dramatically in dialogue and where the positions, movements and relationships of the characters—whether they are alone or in a room with other people or out walking or travelling— are so graphically drawn, and convey such a full awareness of other people, their gestures, their expressions and moods. In many scenes, we are led to visualize the figures; they stand before us like actors on a plain and shallow stage, in a clear, defining light.

But this is not theatre *manqué*, as anyone will know who has tried to dramatize the novels. Dialogue which seems perfect to the eye and sounds perfectly on the internal ear, loses something in the speaking; and professional script-writers have foundered on this problem. What we have in Jane Austen is the true *fictional* comedy of manners, which creates the effect of mental theatre, of an imaginative visualization. It is the reader himself who contributes the backcloth of reality to the furniture of Jane Austen's spare, essential detail. The scenes are enriched, as no performance can be, by the author's frame of commentary and the angle of vision, as, for example, the wholly dramatic dialogue between Mr and Mrs Bennet, in the first chapter of *Pride and*

Prejudice, is sharply framed by the opening lines, the aphoristic pearl of worldly wisdom, 'It is a truth universally acknowledged, that a single man in possession of a good fortune must be in want of a wife'. Then follows an immediate shift, descending from the realms of universal bathos to the banality of a grubby neighbourhood view:

However little known the feelings or views of such a man may be on first entering a neighbourhood, this truth is so well fixed in the minds of the surrounding families, that he is considered as the rightful property of some one or other of their daughters.

The effect is of a camera panning in from outer space, to fasten on a single spot, telescopically enlarged, as chapter I places 'this truth' so solidly and comically before us in the person of Mrs Bennet, fired by the arrival of Mr Bingley, 'a single man of large fortune', within calling-distance of her household of marriageable daughters. Her husband is tired, has heard it all before, plays dumb, draws her on, mocks her. The comedy of repartee is hard and precise. It turns on the twin forces of money and marriage, upon the weary, sardonic, baiting sarcasm of Mr Bennet and the stupid single-mindedness of his wife, 'a woman of mean understanding', whose 'business' in life 'was to get her daughters married'.

The comedy of manners thrives best in a climate of social uneasiness and change, when people are preoccupied with the cultivation of manners, the pursuit of fashion and the show of respectability. Regency England provided just that situation, with its small and compact layer of middle-class gentry (estimated at about 25,000 families). Although the country was at war almost continuously from 1793 until 1814, middle-class life went on virtually unaffected. But structurally it was not a static society. The crucial distinction of gentlemanly birth was disappearing. The lower middle classes were becoming prosperous. Successful farmers, merchants, manufacturers, tradesmen and lawyers were ambitious to share the social standing of the gentry, as far as that could be achieved—by money, by mixing with them, by imitating their manners and their ways of speech. They could be 'gentlemanlike', could behave with 'civility', could start to drink tea in their summer-houses and have parlours, as the Martins dare to do in *Emma*, can dare, like Mrs Elton, the daughter of a Bristol merchant, to act 'the Lady Patroness' of the neighbourhood, usurping the place of Emma Woodhouse, the daughter of the neighbourhood's first gentleman. For young women, fashionable respectability meant being able to play the piano, to sing snatches of French and Italian, to know the gems of English verse, to be knowledgeable about the picturesque, to reel off the titles of the latest novels. These are the fashionable 'accomplishments' that Jane Austen exposes and itemizes. Music, literature and art were reduced to being the trappings of a culture specifically social, components in a shallow display, put on for the sake of polite gentility and ornamental wifeliness.

The snobberies of rank became even sharper during the time that Jane Austen was writing, one of the things she may have had in mind when she added the 'Advertisement' to *Northanger Abbey*. Bath of the 1790s had been a social mixing-pot. Everyone jostled together in the Public Rooms of the Spa. This is how such a nonentity as a Catherine Morland, the unremarkable daughter of an obscure country clergyman, could meet a Henry Tilney, the son of a great landowner; and how both of them could meet the Thorpes, the children of a rising lawyer. In the post-war Bath of *Persuasion*, their paths would never have crossed. By that time, the gentry had left the Public Rooms and entertained in private. A Tilney would have passed his time with one social set, a Morland in another.

Writing for a contemporary audience, Jane Austen's social notation is swift and economical. Money and rank place people on the social map as precisely as a grid reference. It is enough for Jane Austen to tell the reader that Mr Bingley's fortune is £100,000, his sisters' dowries £20,000 each, and that this money is inherited from a father in 'trade' in the north. This signals a family on the way up. The sisters have very superior airs. They patronize the Bennets, disapprove of Elizabeth's 'most country town indifference to decorum' in walking three miles through the mud to visit her sick sister, to arrive with her cheeks a 'blowsy' and unladylike red from the wind. Their 'darling wish' is to see their brother further respectabilize the family by the purchase of a landed estate, which he does.

Jane Austen pairs Bingley with Darcy. He too comes from the north. But there the resemblance ends. His name alone announces an aristocratic Anglo-Norman lineage, a far cry from the plebeian Yorkshire thud of 'Bingley'. He belongs to one of the ancient families of England. His income of £10,000 a year from family estates establishes him as one of a select group of only four hundred such landowners in the whole country. Although he has no title and is technically not a member of the aristocracy, his blood and wealth would make him *persona grata* at the highest levels. So Jane Austen's readers would savour the full comedy of his presence in the dingy small-town atmosphere of Meryton, with its *petite bourgeoisie* of tradesmen, merchants and working lawyers.

Jane Austen had no illusions about the society she lived in. She could see its shallownesses and superficialities and she let them speak for themselves. That Bingley was a northerner with a northern name, a *nouveau riche* of lowly origin, meant nothing to her. She records the data. He is part of the social scene and this is the way in which society would assess him. He has a function in the story and in the pattern of relationships. His extrovert warmth and friendliness, his ease in company, and his other social virtues, provide a foil to Darcy's introvert coldness and unsociability. But Jane Austen passes judgement on Bingley's human worth, not on his social pleasantry, on the fact, for example, that his 'manners' have 'something better than politeness; there was good humour and kindness'.

The novels provide us with a historically accurate picture of a society under stress, its values and its groups in a state of change. The picture is dynamic, analytical and evaluative, as well as descriptive. The pejorative meaning of 'vulgar' and 'vulgarity' is a gentlemanly coinage, to identify and put down the lowness of the lower middle classes and their manners. Jane Austen takes these words and breaks them open. Technically, Mrs Jennings is vulgar. She is a cockney, the widow of a man who traded in an unfashionable part of London. She tramples on every protocol, transgresses every rule of polite behaviour. She is emotionally vulgar, coarsely insensitive, a burden to the Dashwood sisters with her sly hints and loud whispers of suitors, lovers and marriage. She is comically vulgar in her imbecilic fancy that as a glass of Constantia wine cured her husband's 'old cholicky gout', so will it mend Marianne's broken heart. But her 'blunt sincerity' and warm-hearted innocent kindliness towards Marianne redeem everything. Jane Austen does not ask us to forget her vulgarity—it happened and it hurt people; nor does she ask us to discount this vulgarity against Mrs Jennings's motherliness. What she does do is to present us with a woman in whom these qualities and defects stand together in a critical relationship. 'Vulgarity' takes on a new meaning once we have read *Sense and Sensibility*. And a further meaning still when we encounter the brand of vulgarity displayed by Isabella Thorpe, an energetic social climber, who behaves to Catherine Morland as a treacherous and spiteful bitch.

There is also the vulgarity of the gentry. Isabella's transparent deceit is trivial alongside the hollowness of General Tilney's urbane and charming courtesies; and nothing that she does to Catherine Morland can match his callousness in sending the girl home in disgrace from Northanger Abbey. Lady Catherine de Bourgh is aristocratic in name and nature, but an arch-snob, she is supremely vulgar towards her social inferiors. Emma Woodhouse suffers from snobbish, vulgarizing fantasies. Without knowing Robert Martin, she caricatures him as a straw-chewing yokel, 'clownish', 'gross', uncouth and ill-mannered. This is her notion of yeoman farmers. But when she meets him, she discovers a man who is quiet, neat, sensible and well-mannered. He writes a good letter. He even reads the same books as she does! Darcy's 'prejudice' produces the same vulgarizing slant. Until he gets to know them, Elizabeth's uncle and aunt, the Gardiners, belong to the unvisitable, unknowable world of her 'lowly connexions'. In trade, they live within sight of their warehouse in a part of London that a Darcy wouldn't be seen in. But in the flesh he finds them pleasant and likeable; and although the Gardiners are unimportant as characters, Jane Austen bothers to underline his discovery in the last sentences of *Pride and Prejudice*: 'With the Gardiners, they were always on the most intimate terms. Darcy, as well as Elizabeth, really loved them....'

VII

Jane Austen's comedy of manners is a comedy of meanings. Language is behaviour; and the conventional, clichéd language of Regency society is an expression of the people themselves. Jane Austen identified both the slang of fashionable social culture and what she called the 'novel-slang' of its literature. In *Northanger Abbey*, Henry Tilney takes Catherine to task for her use of 'nice' and complains about its loss of meaning.

'Oh! it is a very nice word indeed!—it does for everything. Originally perhaps it was applied only to express neatness, propriety, delicacy, or refinement;—people were nice in their dress, in their sentiments, or their choice. But now every commendation on every subject is comprised in that one word.'

Jane Austen could have repeated this lecture many times over. The strength and discrimination of language that Johnson inherited from Swift and Pope, and before them, from Dryden, Milton and the metaphysical poets, had by this time been dissipated in the rhetoric of sentimental and moralizing fiction. Words passed from writer to writer like worn coins, a currency with an accepted face-value, but its meanings blurred and thin.

The semantic drama of *Sense and Sensibility*, *Pride and Prejudice* and *Persuasion* is signalled in their titles; and within the novels we can follow the scheme of characterization that brings the meaning of these words to life in the complexities and contradictions of human nature. Jane Austen denies the black-and-white morality of conduct fiction. 'Sense' can be as tiresome or as dangerous as 'sensibility'. 'Pride' and 'prejudice' can be strengths as well as weaknesses. 'Persuasion' can be interference. Other words are tested and searched— 'principle', 'judgement', 'improvement', 'propriety'. There is a prominent cluster of social words—'civil', 'civility', 'civilities', 'civilly', 'uncivil', 'incivility'—relating to the principles of etiquette, of meeting the social obligations of politeness, an issue upon which Jane Austen builds a wide ranging conflict between compromise and integrity. These terms are not fixed and passive counters. *Pride and Prejudice* gives 'civility' a very personal meaning. It is the quality that Elizabeth and Darcy have to acquire to temper their superiority and aggressiveness. Her brilliance of mind and sharpness of tongue, his arrogant patricianism, threaten to isolate them from other people. So for them, 'civility' means adjustment, tolerance, sympathy and understanding. 'Duty' is a key-word in *Mansfield Park* and *Persuasion*. In the later eighteenth century it had come to carry the most solemn overtones of moral obligation and religious observance. Jane Austen takes nothing on trust; the word is flooded with a dispassionate irony. Its force as a moral absolute of Christianity is slyly questioned in the sententious invocations of Sir Thomas and Edmund Bertram. In *Persuasion*, an over-developed sense of filial duty brings Anne Elliot years of needless suffering. Duty is what you make it, what you want it to be. At the age of twenty-one, Maria Bertram 'was beginning to think matrimony a duty'; and as there is a young man conveniently at hand, with a grand country house and a princely income of £12,000 a year, 'it became, by the same rule of moral obligation, her evident duty to marry Mr Rushworth if she could'.

The semantic energies of Jane Austen's language are as powerful as the characters and human situations to which they are attached. They are mobilized within a total structure of meaning, a field of force capable of exerting the most delicate vibrations of feeling and tone, and of adumbrating the entire range of social and cultural usage that the language brings in from outside. The novels can be regarded as semantic organisms, analytical works of art that test and display the very language they are composed of; and the novelist herself belongs to that small group of writers for whom language is not only the medium of literature but a part of its subject.

VIII

The underlying theme of Jane Austen's social comedy is the predicament of being a woman in a man's world—a world ruled by men and run for their advantage, in which marriage looms as the central and decisive act of the woman's life, and where the prevailing view is (to quote Coleridge) that 'Marriage has . . . no *natural* relation to love. Marriage belongs to society; it is a social contract'. Other than marriage, no career or occupation was open to her. Her education was a grooming for polite society, providing her with fashionable 'accomplishments' to catch the eye of a future husband. The alternatives were unthinkable. To be a governess was to sell yourself into the slavery of superior servanthood. Jane Austen put it neatly in a letter: 'Single women have a dreadful propensity for being poor—which is one very strong argument in favour of matrimony'. The force of this idea is conjured up in Emma Woodhouse's fearful image of the elderly spinster ridiculed by the children of the village. At worst, then, marriage could be the solution to an economic and human problem, as Jane Austen presents it in *Pride and Prejudice*: 'the only honourable provision for well-educated young women of small fortune, and however uncertain of giving happiness, must be their pleasantest preservative from want'. This sardonic generalization is attached to Charlotte Lucas in her choice of Mr Collins. Elizabeth Bennet is saddened that her friend should humiliate herself with such a man, should 'have sacrificed every better feeling to worldly advantage'. But Charlotte makes this choice with her eyes open. She is twenty-seven, on the verge of becoming 'an old maid'. 'I am not romantic', she tells Elizabeth, 'I never was. I ask only a comfortable home.'

There were other pressures towards marriage, the right marriage, a marriage acceptable to the family, whose status and respectability were defined by the networks of relationship and association established through marriage. For the traditional landowning gentry, these values were vital to the framework of society and their own survival. The crushing force of this system is expounded succinctly in the opening pages of *Sense and Sensibility*, with a history of the Dashwood estate, its preservation from generation to generation through the elaborate legalities of inheritance and succession. The measured rhetoric of the exposition asserts the weight and solidity of the system and the need to maintain the respectability of a family name. It is a system that calls for individual sacrifice. One of the recent Dashwoods was unable to provide for 'those who were most dear to him' by selling any part of the estate, so tight was the knot of its legal bondage. Within this large social-historical image is embodied the ideology of property, its power and mystique, set at the opening of the novel to guide our understanding of the relationship between the individual and society dramatized in the story of Marianne Dashwood. An individualist, a rebel against convention, she has her own romantic 'systems', 'systems' which 'have all the unfortunate tendency of setting propriety at nought', declares Elinor, the censorious voice of social 'sense'. Marianne is eventually tamed and disciplined into behaving politely and dutifully as a young lady should, turning her back on visions of romantic love, and yoked in marriage to the respectable middle-aged suitor promoted by her family and friends—Coleridge's 'social contract' to the letter!

In *Sense and Sensibility*, Jane Austen shows a woman broken by these pressures; in *Pride and Prejudice* she shows how a woman can triumph over them. In this case, it is not the force of the heroine's own family but the weight of 'family' snobbery, pride of caste from the man's side, from Darcy himself and his aunt. This comes to a head in chapter LVI, in one of the great comic scenes of English literature, where Lady Catherine confronts Elizabeth in an attempt to warn her off, facing her with the weighty dynastic claims of the Darcys against the vulgar upstartism of the Bennets.

'Hear me in silence. My daughter and my nephew are formed for each other. They are descended on the maternal side, from the same noble line; and, on the father's, from respectable, honourable, and ancient, though untitled families. Their fortune on both sides is splendid. They are destined for each other by the voice of every member of their respective houses; and what is to divide them? The upstart pretensions of a young woman without family, connexions, or fortune. Is this to be endured! But it must not, shall not be. If you were sensible of your own good, you would not wish to quit the sphere, in which you have been brought up.'

This is comic melodrama, part of a wonderfully contrived scene. Lady Catherine's swelling indignation is pricked by Elizabeth's quiet contempt. Pope would have envied the artistry of Jane Austen's mock-heroics—Lady Catherine thundering with Biblical eloquence, 'Heaven and earth!—of what are you thinking? Are the shades of Pemberley to be thus polluted?'—and the skill of their deflation. But Lady Catherine's bombast is not all hot air. Its hard core is an argument whose authority comes from centuries of social theory and practice. She calls upon ancient sanctities: the dogma of order and hierarchy, whereby the harmony of the whole depends upon the human atoms keeping to their divinely ordained and fixed positions, the great to remain great in the company of their peers, the 'young woman without family, connexions, or fortune' to stay put in the 'sphere' in which she has 'been brought up'.

Elizabeth's social offence is to have her eyes on Darcy. Her offence, as a woman, is to dare to stand up and assert herself as a person, to think for herself, to hold opinions, and to expose herself as an individual with a will of her own. The woman's accepted role was to be passive and submissive. Her function was to be decorative in society, comforting at home, an appendage to the man. Henry Tilney puts the idea playfully to Catherine Morland: 'man has the advantage of choice, woman only the power of refusal . . . he is to purvey, and she is to smile'. The idea takes a more serious turn in the words of Anne Elliot to Captain Harville on the woman's experience of love:

We certainly do not forget you, so soon as you forget us. It is perhaps, our fate rather than our merit. We cannot help ourselves. We live at home, quiet, confined, and our feelings prey upon us. You are forced upon exertion. You have always a profession, pursuits, business of some sort or other, to take you back into the world immediately, and continual occupation and change soon weaken impressions.

In Anne's reference to 'our fate' there is no hint of rhetoric, no false note. Her own life has given her the right to use these words. The bitter truth of separation, loss and remembrance she knows only too well, and she touches on them here with dignity and restraint. Again, there is no hint of rhetoric when Emma Woodhouse reflects on 'the difference of woman's destiny', comparing the social eminence of the great Mrs Churchill and the nonentity of Jane Fairfax, soon to enter the 'governess-trade', 'the sale—not quite of human flesh—but of human intellect'. Jane Austen is expressing the woman's cause but in a way which is totally unpolemical, totally undoctrinaire. The urgent tones of Mary Wollstonecraft and the other crusading feminists of the time only get into the novels as a parody-echo, in the pert aggressiveness of Mrs Elton's warning to Mr Weston:

'I always take the part of my own sex. I do indeed. I give you notice—You will find me a formidable antagonist on that point. I always stand up for women—'

Jane Austen's standing up for women is not argumentative but dramatic. It is implicit in the creation of heroines whose claim to existence is human, whose reality comes from their self-awareness, their possession of minds and feelings, and not as a result of their conformity to some stereotype in either fashionable life or fashionable literature.

When Captain Wentworth asserts that naval vessels are no place for ladies, Mrs Croft corrects him sharply: 'But I hate to hear you talking so, like a fine gentleman, and as if we were all fine ladies, instead of rational creatures'. When Mr Collins refuses to credit Elizabeth's rejection, she has to reprimand him in the same terms: 'Do not consider me now as an elegant female intending to plague you, but as a rational creature speaking the truth from her heart'. Their rationality is something that these women have to argue for in the face of male attitudes which are not so much a consequence of prejudice or stupidity but of habit, a block much more difficult to shift. When the Dashwood sisters are locked in argument, the contest is real; they are not the author's ventriloquial dummies. Marianne is a romantic, passionate woman, but she is far from mindless. Jane Austen underlines Anne Elliot's 'strong mind', her 'maturity of mind', phrases we might think superfluous, since these qualities are so evident in all she does. In this emphatic labelling, we can glimpse Jane Austen's anxiety to press home to her Regency public the message that a woman could have qualities traditionally a man's and that a woman could surpass him in maturity and understanding, as Anne surpasses Wentworth and everyone else in *Persuasion*.

There was indeed a battle to be fought. In *Mansfield Park*, Sir Thomas Bertram comes down heavily on Fanny Price for refusing to accept Henry Crawford. Given the young man's interest and eligibility, the woman's consent is taken for granted. So her refusal is momentous, unnatural, arouses him to an angry diatribe against the new unfeminine 'independence of spirit, which prevails so much in modern days, even in young women, and which in young women is offensive and disgusting beyond all common offence'. Lady Catherine sees this new spirit in Elizabeth Bennet. In her, it is something deliberate and self-conscious, a part of her attraction for Darcy, which she is eager to discuss with him. In Jane Austen's new brand of intellectual romance, the lady can even invite her beloved to analyse the bonds of affection! At the end of the story, she wants him 'to account for his having ever fallen in love with her'; and she is just as keen to present her view of the affair: 'The fact is, that you were sick of civility, of deference, of officious attention. You were disgusted with the women who were always speaking and looking, and thinking for *your* approbation alone. I roused, and interested you, because I was so unlike *them*.' Lady Catherine interpreted her nephew's interest as a sexual infatuation, the sordid outcome of Elizabeth's 'arts and allurements'. Her suspicions are correct; but only half correct. What attracted Darcy was the challenge of a woman whose vitality and presence is intellectual as well as physical.

Each of the heroines presents a different face to the world and is attractive to men for different reasons. None of them can match Elizabeth's high spirits, her aggressive outspokenness and sheer argumentative brilliance. But they are all alike in their possession of an interior life, a dimension of psychological reality, which forms an area of action as important as the action outside and which is drawn with equal care and precision. Jane Austen's method is not stream-of-consciousness nor an elaborate psychoanalytical psychologizing. Her technique is essentially realistic in connecting the ebb and flow of experience to the circumstances of the story and to the heroine's immediate situation. Its credibility comes partly from the thoughtful, reflective nature of the heroines, partly from the train of events, and partly from the fact that the patterns of thought and feeling are so patently normal and recognizable.

While visiting the newly-wed Collins, Elizabeth Bennet has plenty of time to digest the contents of Darcy's second letter, as she goes on solitary walks to escape the company of Mr Collins and Lady Catherine:

After wandering along the lane for two hours, giving way to every variety of thought; re-considering events, determining probabilities, and reconciling herself as well as she could, to a change so sudden and so important, fatigue, and a recollection of her long absence, made her at length return home; and she entered the house with the wish of appearing cheerful as usual, and the resolution of repressing such reflections as must make her unfit for conversation.

Elizabeth's mental and emotional existence is here traced as an active and conscious state of mind. Its progression is geared to the sequence of her movements; and through this technique, Jane Austen is able to convey the *processes* of thought and feeling as well as their quality and content.

There is often a precise enumeration of the levels of experience, the ways in which the same impression can be registered differently, sometimes contradictorily. When Marianne Dashwood hears the news of Lucy Steele's marriage, 'To her own heart it was a delightful affair, to her imagination it was even a ridiculous one, but to her reason, her judgement, it was completely a puzzle'. The impact of feeling can be registered in moral terms. At Portsmouth, Fanny Price was 'quite shocked' by a squabble in the family: 'Every feeling of duty, honour, and tenderness was wounded by her sister's speech and her mother's reply.' Jane Austen's drive is continually discriminative, towards a clarity of mind which is moral as well as rational, towards judgement based upon clear thinking and right feeling. Fanny receives a 'stab' when she concludes that Edmund Bertram's marriage to Mary Crawford is inevitable. She grieves to see someone she loves like a brother caught in the toils of a seductress whom she detests. She is heartbroken, dejected, but rallies herself and determines to 'endeavour to be rational, and to deserve the right of judging Miss Crawford's character and the privilege of true solicitude for him by a sound intellect and an honest heart'.

Jane Austen sets a high value on self-knowledge and each of the novels can be analysed in terms of the heroine's progress along this path. But self-knowledge on its own is not enough and Jane Austen joins to it the idea of a second kind of knowledge, knowledge of our duty in life. This concept appears in *Mansfield Park* where Edmund Bertram sends Mary Crawford off with an admonitory reference to 'the most valuable knowledge we could any of us acquire— the knowledge of ourselves and of our duty'. And his father, Sir Thomas, comes to the conclusion that the sexual mis- behaviour of his daughters must be put down to the fact that in their upbringing 'active principle, had been wanting, that they had never been properly taught to govern their inclinations and tempers, by that sense of duty which can alone suffice'. At the end of *Persuasion*, Anne Elliot is able to congratulate herself on having done the right thing, eight years before, in following Lady Russell's advice by giving up any idea of marrying Wentworth. Lady Russell stood in the place of a mother and, dutifully, as a child, she obeyed. So her conscience remained clear, even if her heart was broken, and she is in a position to reflect: 'If I mistake not, a strong sense of duty is no bad part of a woman's portion'.

These concepts of duty are not presented to us uncritically. Sir Thomas and Edmund both deliver judgement; they enjoy putting other people right and fault-finding in themselves; and there is a glib and defensive rationalization in Anne Elliot's conclusion. But these qualifications are local. The idea of duty was important to Jane Austen, not just the formal duties of religion and family, but the internal duty of individual women towards themselves. To thyself be true. It is this concern which ultimately connects us with Jane Austen, which enables us to understand the heroines in their struggle for individuality and fulfilment, a theme at the heart of nineteenth- and twentieth-century literature, from the Romantic poets onwards; and at the heart, too, of the slow social revolution in England that followed the political revolutions of America and France. In *A Vindication of the Rights of Women*, published in 1792, Mary Wollstonecraft had argued radically that women should not seek 'power over men; but over themselves'; that they should fight free from the degradation of being regarded as mere sexual and social objects, not by overturning society but by valuing themselves as individuals with a right to fulfil themselves in their own way. This message sounds again at the end of *A Doll's House* in Nora's challenge to Torvald. Above the responsibilities of marriage and motherhood, she sees other duties:

Nora: My duties towards myself.
Torvald: Before all else you are a wife and a mother.
Nora: That I no longer believe. I think that before all else I am a human being, just as much as you are—or, at least, I should try to become one. I know that most people agree with you, Torvald, and that they say so in books. But henceforth I can't be satisfied with what most people say, and what is in books. I must think things out for myself and try to get clear about them.

'Let other pens dwell on guilt and misery', Jane Austen began the final chapter of *Mansfield Park*. She declares herself 'impatient to restore everybody, not greatly in fault themselves, to tolerable comfort, and to have done with all the rest'. Without exception, the novels close on a note of dismissive irony, with a rapid tying-up of loose ends. Jane Austen never follows her heroines into the reality of marriage; nor does she carry them to the bitter and tragic point that Nora reaches, where life falls apart and has to be put together again, slowly, painfully and alone. Nevertheless, the comic mask is only a mask. Her heroines' experiences and the meaning of their lives, as much as we are shown of them, are touched with an irony beyond laughter.

In the Foreword to *Women in Love*, Lawrence declared the importance of man's 'struggle for verbal consciousness'. It is

Nora's struggle, her fight to escape from the doll's house in which Torvald has locked her; before her, it is the struggle of Jane Austen's heroines; and today many modern men and women would accept it as their struggle too. Lawrence's enunciation of this process touches the very centre of Jane Austen's art and it helps us to understand the depth of our engagement with the compelling force of these 'verbal' heroines and the 'verbal' structures in which they have their life:

Any man of real individuality tries to know and to understand what is happening, even in himself, as he goes along. This struggle for verbal consciousness should not be left out in art. It is a very great part of life. It is not superimposition of a theory. It is the passionate struggle into conscious being.

IX

Jane Austen's verbalism is most crucially exposed in the treatment of love. In this area, the logic is relentless. Coleridge's axiom—'Marriage has . . . no *natural* relation to love'—defines the premiss of Jane Austen's husband-and-wife comedy. The married couples duly exhibit the gamut of comic symptoms—from lovelessness and boredom to irritation aged into resentment. But the novels also deliver a stern counter-axiom: that marriage does have a *moral* relation to love; and by that test the quality of marriage is to be judged, with the equally decisive qualification that love is not necessarily related to passion or to the feelings conventionally regarded as romantic. For the heroines, a part of love is the recognition of their own needs—Fanny Price for an elder brother, Emma Woodhouse for a kindly, admonitory uncle, the broken Marianne Dashwood for a father-protector. The discovery of mutual affinities, sympathies and understandings is the justification for marriage on human and moral grounds, as distinct from the worldly contracts made for profit or convenience, or the 'social contract' marriages made for the sake of the family. Love is an awareness of the other person, sharpened by judgement into a learning experience. At the close of *Pride and Prejudice*, *Emma* and *Persuasion*, the heroes and heroines are brought even closer together as they talk about the ways in which they have affected one another morally and intellectually, as well as emotionally. This is the final stage in their process of mutual education. These scenes present a remarkable combination of analysis and personal contact in which the sense of emotional intimacy is deepened in the act of discussion.

But what of love as passion? When the couples come together in the full recognition of their feelings, Jane Austen is discretion itself—we are not to intrude upon such tender scenes, not to overhear lovers' talk. Edward Ferrar's declaration is made 'very prettily'. George Knightley delivers himself 'in plain, unaffected, gentlemanlike English'. The 'happiness' Fanny Price inspires in Edmund Bertram is conjectured to 'have been great enough to warrant any strength of language in which he could cloathe it to her or to himself'. Darcy 'expressed himself on the occasion as sensibly and as warmly as a man violently in love can be supposed to do'. Only in *Persuasion* is Jane Austen more forthcoming. The reconciliation of Anne and Wentworth, which leads on without interruption to their declaration of love, is drawn with a richness and intensity of feeling unequalled in the novels. Yet even here, the emphasis remains verbal, the reporting oblique. Their deepest contact is through 'words enough . . . the power of conversation . . . those retrospections and acknowledgements, and especially in those explanations of what had directly preceded the present moment, which were so poignant and so ceaseless of interest'.

Here, as so often in the novels, Jane Austen renders the experience of people discovering and exploring their love for one another, simply through being together, through awarenesses and understandings, spoken and unspoken. This is their making love. If we accept the playful irony of style, the narrator's pose of mock-discretion, Darcy's warmth and the violence of his love are not in question. They are proposed to us, verbally, as qualities to take on trust, part of a mild joke against lovers in general. But in the flesh, there is no warmth or violence of love whatsoever in Darcy. He admires a good figure, but no more than that. This absence from *Pride and Prejudice* and from the relationships in all the later novels is something we have to question if our reading of Jane Austen has begun with *Sense and Sensibility*. For Marianne Dashwood is a woman passionately in love, a woman whose attractiveness and vitality has a genuinely sensuous vibration, and in Willoughby she is matched by a man who has the power to disturb women. Elinor finds her judgement endangered by his presence and the physical aspects of his hold over her are spelt out.

Elinor's problem was also Jane Austen's. She too was disturbed by the power of sexuality, its threat to the security of reason and self-control, its melting attack upon the certainties of selfhood and identity (a point that Lawrence hints at). The tension is evident in *Sense and Sensibility*. The writer's engagement in Marianne and Willoughby is unmistakable. Their destruction—Willoughby blackened with a murky past, the thin and distant melodrama of having seduced a seventeen-year-old schoolgirl! Marianne devitalized through illness and cast off as a 'reward' to the patient Colonel Brandon—is gratuitous and forced, a betrayal of the novel's dramatic commitment, however neatly and maliciously their punishment completes the scheme in which the sickness of 'sensibility' is purged with a stiff dose of 'sense'. After this exercise in suppression, Jane Austen tried to turn her back on the problem. Her heroes are a dull and unvirile crew; her heroines are untroubled by passion. Sexuality is outlawed, reserved for the villains and villainesses and the silly little girls and the married women who should know better: for Wickham and Lydia, who were 'only brought together because their passions were stronger than their virtue'; for the Crawfords, whose dangerous, seductive charm has to be smeared with the taint of corruption (again, some readers have felt, gratuitously). Whatever the solid virtues of George Knightley, whatever the truth-to-life in his marriage to Emma Woodhouse, there is some shadowy objection to his avuncular and tutelary union to a girl of such brilliance, beauty and the 'bloom of full health'. *Persuasion* is *Sense and Sensibility* safely rewritten, with the rational 'romance' of maturity, and quieter, more tender, poetic charms substituted for the impulsive infatuation of youth.

Charlotte Brontë wondered where in Jane Austen is 'that stormy Sisterhood . . . the Passions'. It is a question that has been raised by many of Jane Austen's critics; it lurks within Lawrence's 'narrow-gutted spinster'. One answer is in *Sense and Sensibility*, which Charlotte Brontë had not read. Marianne Dashwood is a heroine whose courage and love she would have applauded and whose suffering she would have wept for; and surely Lawrence would have cheered her too, if ever he had read the book with an open mind. The other answer is that Jane Austen tried to undercut the passions with irony, to detach herself from them, and to subject them to the pressure of her own compelling need for order and control, the driving necessity of her imagination and her whole being, the force which stands behind the achievement of the novels both in their scope and their limitations.

X

As far as her fellow-countrymen are concerned, Jane Austen can properly be described as the most *beloved* of English novelists. Like Shakespeare, she has transcended literary greatness, to become part of our national heritage and something of a cult. Her anniversaries are commemorated, her homes are visited, and Chawton Cottage is preserved by the Jane Austen Society as a place of pilgrimage. Strictly speaking, these circumstances have more to do with social anthropology than literary criticism. But the fact remains that of all the great English novelists, Jane Austen is the only one to survive into the 1970s with such a devoted following. Her works are known with more intimacy than those of Shakespeare himself. If he is revered as our national poet, Jane Austen is loved as our national novelist, the most widely enjoyed and in many ways the most English of all English writers.

Generations of readers have treasured the novels nostalgically. They seem to immortalize a golden age in English society, ('the last voice of a happier age' commented V. S.

Pritchett). There are still people in this country who can identify themselves and their acquaintances, charitably and uncharitably, with Jane Austen's characters and their way of life. For them, the novels can be potently authenticating, as they were for their Regency audience. There is a special pleasure, the joy of recognition, in discovering oneself drawn so accurately and artistically. Like family portraits and domestic interiors of a Dutch fidelity, they flatter by the very perfection of the rendering. The basis of Jane Austen's social comedy has not dated, with its attention to manners and the refinements of social behaviour, its play upon vulgarity and the distinctions of class. The forms have changed, but the system remains, and for those who live within it the novels can be read as a celebration of traits that are cherished as typically and endearingly English—our insularity, our bluff and determined philistinism, our anti-intellectualism, our wariness of Mediterranean passion and French gallantry, our sense of order, decorum and self-control, our anxieties about social background and breeding, our respect for duty, propriety and tradition, and, the ultimate saving grace of the English, our thick-skinned capacity to laugh at ourselves and so draw the sting of any joke.

Nostalgic, wishful, chauvinistic and unliterary, jealous, possessive and snobbish, this view of the novels is partial, blind to their irony and to the force of their social judgement. Nonetheless, it is a view which has been held firmly and continuously in this country from Jane Austen's own time until the present day. Its voice can still be heard and occasionally breaks into print. In the summer of 1974, when a current domestic worry was the rising price of bread, this short letter appeared in the correspondence columns of one of our national papers:

Sir,
    We hear a lot about the cost of bread and even the shortage of this essential commodity. There is a perfectly simple answer which is to bake one's own bread; we have done this for years and my cook produces much finer bread than you can obtain in the ordinary way. It is also much cheaper and requires no expensive equipment.

Jane Austen would have greeted the unconscious irony of this letter with a smile of recognition. Bread was expensive in her day too; and there was no shortage of advice from the gentry, just as well-meaning, suggesting how the poor could feed themselves economically.

According to Hobbes, 'laughter is a bad infirmity of human nature which every thinking man will attempt to overcome'. The novels of Jane Austen offer a different moral, that laughter comes to our rescue, is a necessary strength, a realistic response, an understanding, which enables 'thinking' people to hold out in the face of life's irrational and chaotic ironies. Jane Austen's vision would place her far along Nietzsche's scale of laughing philosophers, by which they are ordered 'according to the rank of their laughter—rising to those capable of *golden* laughter'. In the passage in *Beyond Good and Evil* where he presents this idea, Nietzsche goes on to speculate upon 'the Olympian vice', divine laughter:

And if gods too philosophize, as many an inference has driven me to suppose—I do not doubt that while doing so they know how to laugh in a new and superhuman way—and at the expense of all serious things! Gods are fond of mockery; it seems they cannot refrain from laughter even when sacraments are in progress.

Jane Austen's laughter is directed at the secular sacraments and sacred cows of the Regency world—at its fashionable modes of feeling and thinking, at its idols of class and culture, at its categoricalisms, its rage for order, inherited from the Age of Reason, at its sentimental romanticism, at its litany of 'improvement', 'duty', 'sense', 'civility'. Her laughter is amused, intellectual and sardonic. But there the superhumanism, the Godlike mockery ends. For behind the laughter is sadness and compassion. And behind that is anger and frustration, the tensions of a satirist who uncovers the shams, shabbinesses and inhumanities of her world, its oppressions and claustrophobias, yet who nevertheless belongs to it, needs it, and cannot exist outside it. Its profoundest critic and historian, she is its victim herself.

JANE AUSTEN

A Select Bibliography

(Place of publication London, unless stated otherwise. Detailed biblio-
graphical information will also be found in Vol. III of *The New Cambridge
Bibliography of English Literature*.)

Bibliography:

JANE AUSTEN: A Bibliography, by G. L. Keynes (1929)
—the standard methodical bibliography, published in a limited edition
by the Nonesuch Press. Includes a list of secondary material up to
1928.
JANE AUSTEN: A Critical Bibliography, by R. W. Chapman; Oxford
(1953)
—second edition, 1955. A selective list, with good coverage of historical
and biographical material.

Collected Works:

NOVELS, 5 vols (1833)
—the first collected edition, published by Richard Bentley. Reprinted
1866 and 1869. A volume called *Lady Susan &c* was added to the
edition of 1878-9 containing *A Memoir of Jane Austen*, by her nephew,
J. E. Austen-Leigh, first published separately in 1870.
WORKS, 6 vols (1882)
—the Steventon Edition. Vol. VI contains the *Memoirs* by her nephew,
Lady Susan, and other fragments.
NOVELS, ed. R. B. Johnson, 10 vols (1892)
—illustrated by W. C. Cooke and ornaments by F. C. Tilney.
NOVELS, ed. R. B. Johnson, 10 vols (1898)
—illustrated by C. E. and H. M. Brock.
NOVELS, 10 vols (1898)
—The Winchester Edition.
WORKS, 10 vols (1899)
—The Temple Edition.
NOVELS, 6 vols (1902)
—the Hampshire edition. Decorated by B. MacManus.
WORKS, 6 vols (1907-31)
—with introductions by Lord David Cecil, R. W. Chapman,
M. Lascelles, Michael Sadleir, and Forrest Reid. In the 'World's
Classics' series.

WORKS, ed. R. B. Johnson, 10 vols (1908–9)

—illustrated by A. W. Mills. In the St Martin's Illustrated Library of Standard Authors.

NOVELS, 6 vols (1922)

—introduction by R. B. Johnson. Illustrated by C. E. Brock.

NOVELS: The Text based on Collation of the Early Editions by R. W. Chapman. With Notes, Indexes, and Illustrations from Contemporary Sources. 5 vols; Oxford (1923). Vol. VI, *Minor Works* (1954).

—reprinted (without coloured plates) 1926, (with corrections) 1933, (in two volumes) 1934. The definitive edition, outstanding for its careful scholarship.

WORKS, 7 vols (1923)

—the Adelphi Edition. Vol. VII contains *Lady Susan* and *The Watsons*.

WORKS, 5 vols (1927)

—the Georgian Edition. With an Introduction to each volume by J. C. Bailey which were reprinted in a separate volume, 1931.

THE COMPLETE NOVELS (1928)

—an 'Omnibus' edition in one volume, with an Introduction by J. C. Squire.

NOVELS, 6 vols (1948)

—the Chawton edition.

WORKS, 7 vols (1933–4)

—illustrated by M. Vox. Vol. VII contains *Sanditon*, *The Watsons*, *Lady Susan*, and other miscellanea. Introduction by R. B. Johnson.

[NOVELS], ed. M. M. Lascelles, 5 vols (1961–4)

—in the Everyman library.

[NOVELS], 6 vols (1969–72)

—Penguin English Library.

[NOVELS], 6 vols (1970)

—Oxford English Novels series.

Letters:

LETTERS. Edited with an Introduction and critical remarks, by Edward Lord Brabourne, 2 vols (1884).

JANE AUSTEN'S SAILOR BROTHERS, by J. H. and E. C. Hubback (1906)

—contains unpublished letters to her brother Francis.

JANE AUSTEN: Her Life and Letters, by W. Austen-Leigh and R. A. Austen-Leigh (1913)

—contains numerous extracts from Jane Austen's letters. See below under 'Biographical and Critical Studies'.

FIVE LETTERS FROM JANE AUSTEN TO HER NIECE FANNY KNIGHT, ed. R. W. Chapman; Oxford (1924)

—printed in facsimile.

LETTERS, selected, with an Introduction, by R. B. Johnson (1925).

JANE AUSTEN'S LETTERS TO HER SISTER CASSANDRA AND OTHERS. Collected and edited by R. W. Chapman, 2 vols; Oxford (1932)

—the only complete edition and a definitive text, with notes and indexes. Reprinted in one volume, with additions, 1952. A selection of letters appeared in the World's Classics, 1955.

Separate Works:

SENSE AND SENSIBILITY: A Novel, by a Lady, 3 vols (1811)

—second edition, corrected, 1813.

PRIDE AND PREJUDICE: A Novel, 3 vols (1813).

MANSFIELD PARK: A Novel, 3 vols (1814)

—second edition, corrected, 1816.

EMMA: A Novel, 3 vols (1816).

NORTHANGER ABBEY and PERSUASION, 4 vols (1818)

—contains a biographical notice of the author by her brother, Henry Austen. (Included in Bentley's edition of 1833.)

LADY SUSAN and THE WATSONS (1871). *Unfinished Novels*

—first printed in the second edition, 1871, of *A Memoir of Jane Austen* by her nephew J. E. Austen-Leigh. Reprinted together 1939, with an Introduction by J. Bailey. *The Watsons* was reprinted separately, 1923 (Introduction by A. B. Walkley); 1927 (reprinted from the MS, by R. W. Chapman, Oxford); 1928 (completed by E. and F. Brown, in accordance with her intentions.)

LOVE AND FREINDSHIP [*sic*] and Other Early Works. Now first printed from the original MS; with a Preface by G. K. Chesterton (1922)

—comprises the contents of MSS *Juvenilia*, in the Bodleian Library, Oxford.

[SANDITON]. Fragment of a Novel written January–March 1817. Now first printed from the manuscript. Edited, with Preface, by R. W. Chapman; Oxford (1925)

—reprinted, 1934, with *The Watsons, Lady Susan*, and 'Other Miscellanea', edited by R. B. Johnson.

PLAN OF A NOVEL, ACCORDING TO HINTS FROM VARIOUS QUARTERS. With opinions on *Mansfield Park* and *Emma*, collected and transcribed, and other documents (with facsimiles); Oxford (1926).

TWO CHAPTERS OF 'PERSUASION', ed. R. W. Chapman; Oxford (1926)

—the first draft of chapters X and XI in Vol. II.

VOLUME THE FIRST. Now first printed from the manuscript in the Bodleian Library. Edited with a Preface by R. W. Chapman (with facsimiles); Oxford (1933)

—comprises the contents of the first of three MS notebooks in which Jane Austen collected (*c.* 1793) her *Juvenilia*.

VOLUME THE THIRD. Now first printed from the MS (in the possession of Mr. R. A. Austen-Leigh), edited with a Preface by R. W. Chapman; Oxford (1951)

—the third of Jane Austen's MS notebooks.

VOLUME THE SECOND. [Love and Freindship], ed. B. C. Southam; Oxford (1963).

Some Critical and Biographical Studies:

(*Note: Writers and their Work* does not normally include periodical articles in its Select Bibliographies, but in view of their chronological significance, some articles are given below in sequence. Those marked (L) may be found reprinted in D. Lodge's *Jane Austen: Emma: A Casebook*, 1968, those marked (S) in B. C. Southam's *Jane Austen: The Critical Heritage*, 1968, and those marked (W) in Ian Watt's *Jane Austen: A Collection of Critical Essays*, 1963.)

[Review of *Emma*, by Sir Walter Scott], *Quarterly Review*, XIV, 1815

—the most important contemporary statement. (S)

[Review of *Northanger Abbey* and *Persuasion*, by R. Whately], *Quarterly Review*, XXIV, 1821

—a classic essay. (S)

'The Diary and Letters of Madame D'Arblay', by T. B. Macaulay, *Edinburgh Review*, LXXVI, 1843.

'The Novels of Jane Austen', by G. H. Lewes, *Blackwood's Magazine*, July 1859.

ENGLISH WOMEN OF LETTERS, by J. Kavanagh (1862)

—ch. XVIII, 'Miss Austen's Six Novels'. (S)

A MEMOIR OF JANE AUSTEN, by J. E. Austen-Leigh (1870)

—second edition, 1871, to which were added *Lady Susan*, *The Watsons*, *Sanditon*, *Plan of a Novel*, etc.

[Review of the *Memoir of Jane Austen*, by R. Simpson], *North British Review*, LII, 1870. (S)

JANE AUSTEN AND HER WORKS, by 'S. Tytler' [H. Keddie] (1880).

JANE AUSTEN'S NOVELS, by W. G. Pellew; Boston (1883).

JANE AUSTEN, by S. F. Malden (1889)

—in the 'Eminent Women Series'.

LIFE OF JANE AUSTEN, by G. Smith (1890)

—contains a bibliography by J. P. Anderson.

THE STORY OF JANE AUSTEN'S LIFE, by O. F. Adams; Chicago (1891)

—revised ed., Boston, 1897.

ESSAYS ON THE NOVEL AS ILLUSTRATED BY SCOTT AND MISS AUSTEN, by A. Jack (1897).

JANE AUSTEN, HER CONTEMPORARIES AND HERSELF: An Essay in Criticism, by W. H. Pollock (1899).

HEROINES OF FICTION, by W. D. Howells; New York(1901).

JANE AUSTEN: Her Homes and Her Friends, by C. Hill(1901).

CHARLOTTE BRONTË, GEORGE ELIOT, JANE AUSTEN: Studies in Their
Works, by H. H. Bonnell; New York(1902).

JANE AUSTEN AND HER TIMES, by G. E. Mitton(1905).

JANE AUSTEN'S SAILOR BROTHERS, by J. H. and E. C. Hubback(1906).

INTRODUCTION TO JANE AUSTEN'S NOVELS, by W. L. Phelps(1906).

JANE AUSTEN AND HER COUNTRY-HOUSE COMEDY, by W. H. Helm(1909).

JANE AUSTEN: A Lecture, by A. C. Bradley; Oxford(1911)

—in the English Association's *Essays and Studies*, Vol. II. Reprinted in the
author's *A Miscellany*, 1929.

JANE AUSTEN: A Criticism and an Appreciation, by P. H. Fitzgerald
(1912).

JANE AUSTEN, by M. Sackville(1912).

JANE AUSTEN: Her Life and Letters, A Family Record, by W. Austen-
Leigh and R. A. Austen-Leigh(1913)

—the authoritative biography. An indispensable record, based on
family papers.

JANE AUSTEN, by F. W. Cornish(1913)

—in the 'English Men of Letters' series.

JANE AUSTEN, by K. and P. Rague; Paris(1914)

—in 'Les Grands Écrivains Étrangers' series.

JANE AUSTEN, Sa Vie et Son Oeuvre, 1775–1817, by L. Villard; Lyons
(1915)

—translated in part by V. Lucas, as *Jane Austen: A French Appreciation*,
with a new study of Jane Austen interpreted through *Love and
Freindship* [sic] by R. B. Johnson, 1924.

'Jane Austen', by R. Farrer, *Quarterly Review*, CCXXVIII, 1917.
(extracts in L)

JANE AUSTEN CENTENARY MEMORIAL: A record of the Ceremony of its
Unveiling at Chawton, Hampshire, by Sir F. Pollock(1917).

PERSONAL ASPECTS OF JANE AUSTEN, by M. A. Austen-Leigh(1920).

JANE AUSTEN, by O. W. Firkins; New York(1920).

THE COMMON READER, by V. Woolf (1925)

—contains an appreciation of Jane Austen. (W)

JANE AUSTEN, by R. B. Johnson(1925).

THE NORTHANGER NOVELS: A Footnote to Jane Austen, by M. Sadleir;
Oxford(1927)

—English Association Pamphlet No. 68.

THE ART OF JANE AUSTEN, by S. Alexander; Manchester(1928).

'Jane Austen: A depreciation', by H. W. Garrod, *Transactions of the
Royal Society of Literature*, n.s. VIII, 1928.

JANE AUSTEN: A Survey, by C. L. Thomson(1929).

JANE AUSTEN: Her Life, Her Work, Her Family and Her Critics, by R. B. Johnson (1930).

INTRODUCTIONS TO JANE AUSTEN, by J. C. Bailey (1931).

A JANE AUSTEN DICTIONARY, by G. L. Apperson (1932).

JANE AUSTEN: Her Life and Art, by D. Rhydderch (1932).

JANE AUSTEN, by G. Rawlence (1934).

JANE AUSTEN, by Lord David Cecil; Cambridge (1935)

—the Leslie Stephen Lecture, 1935.

JANE AUSTEN, by E. Bowen (1936)

—in the 'English Novelists' series.

JANE AUSTEN: Study for a Portrait, by B. K. Seymour (1937).

JANE AUSTEN AND STEVENTON, by E. Austen-Leigh (1937).

JANE AUSTEN AND SOME CONTEMPORARIES, by M. Wilson (1938).

JANE AUSTEN: A Biography, by E. Jenkins (1938).

JANE AUSTEN IN BATH, by M. Ragg (1938).

JANE AUSTEN AND BATH, by E. Austen-Leigh (1939).

JANE AUSTEN AND HER ART, by M. M. Lascelles (1939).

—the first systematic study of Jane Austen's achievement. An indispensable introductory essay.

JANE AUSTEN AND LYME REGIS, by E. Austen-Leigh (1940).

'Regulated Hatred: An Aspect of the Work of Jane Austen', by D. W. Harding, *Scrutiny*, VIII, 1940. (W)

TALKING OF JANE AUSTEN, by S. Kaye-Smith and G. B. Stern (1943).

'The Controlling Hand: Jane Austen and *Pride and Prejudice*', by R. Brower, *Scrutiny*, XIII, 1945

—an outstanding essay. Reprinted in his *Fields of Light*, New York, 1951. (W)

JANE AUSTEN AND LYME REGIS, by R. A. Austen-Leigh (1946).

'Jane Austen's *Pride and Prejudice* in the eighteenth-century mode', by S. Kliger, *University of Toronto Quarterly*, XVI, 1947.

JANE AUSTEN: Facts and Problems, by R. W. Chapman; Oxford (1948)

—the Clark Lectures, Trinity College, Cambridge, 1948.

'Jane Austen, Karl Marx and the aristocratic dance', by D. Daiches, *American Scholar*, XVII, 1948.

'Technique as Discovery', by M. Schorer, *Hudson Review*, I, 1948.

JANE AUSTEN AND SOUTHAMPTON, by E. Austen-Leigh (1949).

PARSON AUSTEN'S DAUGHTER, by H. Ashton (1949).

'Fiction and the "matrix of analogy"', by M. Schorer, *Kenyon Review*, XI, 1949.

JANE AUSTEN AND JANE AUSTEN'S HOUSE, by various writers; Winchester (1949).

JANE AUSTEN AND SOUTHAMPTON, by R. A. Austen-Leigh (1949).

MORE TALK OF JANE AUSTEN, by S. Kaye-Smith and G. B. Stern (1950).

JANE AUSTEN, by M. Kennedy (1950).

'*Emma*: A Dissenting opinion', by E. N. Hayes, *Nineteenth-Century Fiction*, IV, 1950. (L)

JANE AUSTEN, by Sylvia Townsend Warner (1951)

—a British Council pamphlet; revised eds., 1957, 1964.

MY AUNT JANE AUSTEN: A Memoir, by Caroline Austen, ed. R. W. Chapman; Alton, Hants (1952)

—from a MS dated March 1867.

JANE AUSTEN: Irony as Defense and Discovery, by M. Mudrick; Princeton (1952).

PRESENTING MISS JANE AUSTEN, by M. L. Becker (1953).

JANE AUSTEN'S NOVELS: A Study in Structure, by A. H. Wright (1953)

—second ed., 1972.

THE ENGLISH NOVEL: Form and Function, by D. Van Ghent; New York (1953)

—includes a chapter 'On *Pride and Prejudice*'.

AN INTRODUCTION TO THE ENGLISH NOVEL, by A. Kettle (1953)

—Vol. I includes an essay, 'Jane Austen: *Emma*'. (W, L)

'A Note on Jane Austen', by C. S. Lewis, *Essays in Criticism*, IV, 1954. (W)

'*Emma*: Character and Construction', by E. F. Shannon, *Publications of the Modern Language Association of America*, LXXI, 1956. (L)

'Pride unprejudiced', by M. Schorer, *Kenyon Review*, XVIII, 1956.

THE RISE OF THE NOVEL: Studies in Defoe, Richardson and Fielding, by Ian Watt (1957)

—the best account of Jane Austen's relationship to the eighteenth-century novel.

THE PELICAN GUIDE TO ENGLISH LITERATURE, Harmondsworth (1957)

—Vol. V: *From Blake to Byron*, Part II includes 'Jane Austen and Moral Judgement', by D. W. Harding.

LITERARY STUDIES, by Lord David Cecil (1957)

—contains notes on *Sense and Sensibility* and Jane Austen's scenery.

[Introduction to] Jane Austen's EMMA, by L. Trilling; New York (1957)

—in the Riverside edition. Essay entitled 'Emma and the Legend of Jane Austen'; reprinted in his *Beyond Culture*, 1965. (L)

'The Context of *Sense and Sensibility*', by A. D. McKillop, *Rice Institute Pamphlets*, XLIV, 1958.

FROM JANE AUSTEN TO JOSEPH CONRAD, ed. R. C. Rathburn and M. Steinmann; Minneapolis (1958)

—includes 'The Background of *Mansfield Park*', by C. Murrah, and 'Critical Realism in *Northanger Abbey*', by A. D. McKillop.

THE WATSONS: Jane Austen's Fragment Continued and Completed, by J. Coates (1958).

'Sense and Sensibility: An assessment', by C. Gillie, *Essays in Criticism*, IX, 1959.

'The Humiliation of Emma Woodhouse', by M. Schorer, *Literary Review*, II, 1959.

THE PARENTS IN JANE AUSTEN'S NOVELS, by J. Hubback; privately printed (1960).

JANE AUSTEN IN LONDON, by W. Watson (1960).

THE RHETORIC OF FICTION, by W. C. Booth (1961)
—includes an essay, 'Control of Distance in Jane Austen's *Emma*'. (L)

JANE AUSTEN: *Emma*, by F. W. Bradbrook (1961).

DISCUSSIONS OF JANE AUSTEN, by W. W. Heath; Boston (1961).

JANE AUSTEN'S NOVELS: The Fabric of Dialogue, by H. S. Babb; Columbus, Ohio (1962).

'The Education of Emma Woodhouse', by R. E. Hughes, *Nineteenth-Century Fiction*, XVI, 1962. (L)

'Jane Austen's *Emma*', by M. Bradbury, *Critical Quarterly*, IV, 1962. (L)

JANE AUSTEN, by S. Ebiike; Tokyo (1962).

THE NOVELS OF JANE AUSTEN, by R. Liddell (1963).

JANE AUSTEN: A Collection of Critical Essays, ed. I. Watt; Englewood Cliffs, N.J. (1963).

JANE AUSTEN'S LITERARY MANUSCRIPTS: A Study of the novelist's development through the surviving papers, by B. C. Southam (1964).

JANE AUSTEN: A Study in Fictional Conventions, by H. Ten Harmsel; The Hague (1964).

THE DREAM AND THE TASK, by G. Hough (1964)
—includes an essay, '*Emma* and "moral" criticism'. (L)

JANE AUSTEN: The Six Novels, by W. A. Craik (1965).

JANE AUSTEN: A Study of her Artistic Development, by A. W. Litz (1965).

JANE AUSTEN AND HER PREDECESSORS, by F. Bradbrook (1966).

JANE AUSTEN AND HER WORLD, by Ivor Brown (1966).

'Jane Austen and the Moralists', by G. Ryle, *Oxford Review*, I, 1966.

JANE AUSTEN, by N. Sherry (1966).

FICTION WITH A PURPOSE, by R. A. Colby (1967)
—ch. III, '*Mansfield Park:* Fanny Price and the Christian Heroine'.

A READING OF 'MANSFIELD PARK': An Essay in critical synthesis, by A. Fleishman; Baltimore (1967)
—the most detailed historical study.

'The Plot of *Emma*', by W. J. Harvey, *Essays in Criticism*, XVII, 1967. (L)

THE TRUTHTELLERS: Jane Austen, George Eliot, D. H. Lawrence, by L. Lerner (1967).

THE ERRAND OF FORM: An assay of Jane Austen's art, by Joseph Wiesenfarth (1967).

JANE AUSTEN: *Emma*: A Casebook, ed. D. Lodge (1968).

JANE AUSTEN'S ART OF ALLUSION, by K. L. Moler; Lincoln, Nebraska (1968).

CRITICAL ESSAYS ON JANE AUSTEN, ed. B. C. Southam (1968).

JANE AUSTEN: The Critical Heritage, ed. B. C. Southam (1968).

JANE AUSTEN AND HER WORLD, by M. Laski (1969).

JANE AUSTEN IN HER TIME, by W. A. Craik (1969).

[Introductions to] Jane Austen's SENSE AND SENSIBILITY and MANSFIELD PARK, by Tony Tanner (1969, 1970)
—in the Penguin English Library edition.

JANE AUSTEN, by Y. Gooneratne; Cambridge (1970).

'Narrative and Dialogue in Jane Austen', by G. Hough, *Critical Quarterly*, Autumn 1970.

CRITICS ON JANE AUSTEN, ed. J. O'Neill (1970).

JANE AUSTEN'S ENGLISH, by Kenneth C. Phillipps (1970).

THE ENGLISH NOVEL FROM DICKENS TO LAWRENCE, by Raymond Williams (1970)
—the Introduction discusses Jane Austen.

THE IMPROVEMENT OF THE ESTATE: a Study of Jane Austen's novels, by A. M. Duckworth; Baltimore (1971).

STYLES IN FICTIONAL STRUCTURE: The Art of Jane Austen, Charlotte Brontë, George Eliot, by Karl Kroeber; Princeton (1971).

'General Tilney's Hot-houses: Some recent Jane Austen studies and texts', by B. C. Southam, *Ariel*, October 1971.

THE DOUBLE LIFE OF JANE AUSTEN, by J. A. Hodge (1972).

THE LANGUAGE OF JANE AUSTEN, by Norman Page; Oxford (1972).

THE OSPREY GUIDE TO JANE AUSTEN, by J. M. D. Hardwick; Reading (1973).

THE NOVELS OF JANE AUSTEN: An Interpretation, by D. Mansell (1973).

A JANE AUSTEN COMPANION: A Critical survey and reference book, by F. B. Pinion (1973).

SOME WORDS OF JANE AUSTEN, by S. M. Tave; Chicago (1973).

WHO'S WHO IN JANE AUSTEN AND THE BRONTËS, by Glenda Leeming (1974).

A PREFACE TO JANE AUSTEN, by C. Gillie (1974).

JANE AUSTEN, by Douglas Bush (1975).

JANE AUSTEN AND THE WAR OF IDEAS, by Marilyn Butler; Oxford (1975).

JANE AUSTEN AND EDUCATION, by D. D. Devlin (1975).

JANE AUSTEN: Bicentenary Essays, ed. John Halperin; Cambridge (1975).

A READING OF JANE AUSTEN, by Barbara Hardy (1975).

JANE AUSTEN: Woman and Writer, by Joan Rees (1976).

HUME: Montgomery Belgion
SAMUEL JOHNSON: S. C. Roberts
POPE: Ian Jack
RICHARDSON: R. F. Brissenden
SHERIDAN: W. A. Darlington
CHRISTOPHER SMART: G. Grigson
SMOLLETT: Laurence Brander
STEELE, ADDISON: A. R. Humphreys
STERNE: D. W. Jefferson
SWIFT: J. Middleton Murry
SIR JOHN VANBRUGH: Bernard Harris
HORACE WALPOLE: Hugh Honour

Nineteenth Century:

MATTHEW ARNOLD: Kenneth Allott
JANE AUSTEN: S. Townsend Warner
BAGEHOT: N. St John-Stevas
THE BRONTËS: I & II: Winifred Gérin
BROWNING: John Bryson
E. B. BROWNING: Alethea Hayter
SAMUEL BUTLER: G. D. H. Cole
BYRON: I, II & III:
                Bernard Blackstone
CARLYLE: David Gascoyne
LEWIS CARROLL: Derek Hudson
COLERIDGE: Kathleen Raine
CREEVEY & GREVILLE: J. Richardson
DE QUINCEY: Hugh Sykes Davies
DICKENS: K. J. Fielding
  EARLY NOVELS: T. Blount
  LATER NOVELS: B. Hardy
DISRAELI: Paul Bloomfield
GEORGE ELIOT: Lettice Cooper
FERRIER & GALT: W. M. Parker
FITZGERALD: Joanna Richardson
ELIZABETH GASKELL: Miriam Allott
GISSING: A. C. Ward
THOMAS HARDY: R. A. Scott-James
                and C. Day Lewis
HAZLITT: J. B. Priestley
HOOD: Laurence Brander
G. M. HOPKINS: Geoffrey Grigson
T. H. HUXLEY: William Irvine
KEATS: Edmund Blunden
LAMB: Edmund Blunden
LANDOR: G. Rostrevor Hamilton
EDWARD LEAR: Joanna Richardson
MACAULAY: G. R. Potter

MEREDITH: Phyllis Bartlett
JOHN STUART MILL: M. Cranston
WILLIAM MORRIS: P. Henderson
NEWMAN: J. M. Cameron
PATER: Ian Fletcher
PEACOCK: J. I. M. Stewart
ROSSETTI: Oswald Doughty
CHRISTINA ROSSETTI: G. Battiscombe
RUSKIN: Peter Quennell
SIR WALTER SCOTT: Ian Jack
SHELLEY: G. M. Matthews
SOUTHEY: Geoffrey Carnall
LESLIE STEPHEN: Phyllis Grosskurth
R. L. STEVENSON: G. B. Stern
SWINBURNE: Ian Fletcher
TENNYSON: B. C. Southam
THACKERAY: Laurence Brander
FRANCIS THOMPSON: P. Butter
TROLLOPE: Hugh Sykes Davies
OSCAR WILDE: James Laver
WORDSWORTH: Helen Darbishire

Twentieth Century:

CHINUA ACHEBE: A. Ravenscroft
JOHN ARDEN: Glenda Leeming
W. H. AUDEN: Richard Hoggart
SAMUEL BECKETT: J-J. Mayoux
HILAIRE BELLOC: Renée Haynes
ARNOLD BENNETT: Kenneth Young
JOHN BETJEMAN: John Press
EDMUND BLUNDEN: Alec M. Hardie
ROBERT BRIDGES: J. Sparrow
ANTHONY BURGESS: Carol M. Dix
ROY CAMPBELL: David Wright
JOYCE CARY: Walter Allen
G. K. CHESTERTON: C. Hollis
WINSTON CHURCHILL: John Connell
R. G. COLLINGWOOD: E. W. F. Tomlin
I. COMPTON-BURNETT:
                R. Glynn Grylls
JOSEPH CONRAD: Oliver Warner
WALTER DE LA MARE: K. Hopkins
NORMAN DOUGLAS: Ian Greenlees
LAWRENCE DURRELL: G. S. Fraser
T. S. ELIOT: M. C. Bradbrook
T. S. ELIOT: The Making of
  'The Waste Land': M. C. Bradbrook

FORD MADOX FORD:
                        Kenneth Young
E. M. FORSTER: Rex Warner
CHRISTOPHER FRY: Derek Stanford
JOHN GALSWORTHY: R. H. Mottram
WILLIAM GOLDING: Stephen Medcalf
ROBERT GRAVES: M. Seymour-Smith
GRAHAM GREENE: Francis Wyndham
L. P. HARTLEY: Paul Bloomfield
A. E. HOUSMAN: Ian Scott-Kilvert
TED HUGHES: Keith Sagar
ALDOUS HUXLEY: Jocelyn Brooke
HENRY JAMES: Michael Swan
PAMELA HANSFORD JOHNSON:
                        Isabel Quigly
JAMES JOYCE: J. I. M. Stewart
RUDYARD KIPLING: Bonamy Dobrée
PHILIP LARKIN: Alan Brownjohn
D. H. LAWRENCE: Kenneth Young
DORIS LESSING: Michael Thorpe
C. DAY LEWIS: Clifford Dyment
WYNDHAM LEWIS: E. W. F. Tomlin
COMPTON MACKENZIE: K. Young
LOUIS MACNEICE: John Press
KATHERINE MANSFIELD: Ian Gordon
JOHN MASEFIELD: L. A. G. Strong
SOMERSET MAUGHAM: J. Brophy
GEORGE MOORE: A. Norman Jeffares
J. MIDDLETON MURRY: Philip Mairet
R. K. NARAYAN: William Walsh
SEAN O'CASEY: W. A. Armstrong

GEORGE ORWELL: Tom Hopkinson
JOHN OSBORNE: Simon Trussler
WILFRED OWEN: Dominic Hibberd
HAROLD PINTER: John Russell Taylor
POETS OF 1939-45 WAR:
                        R. N. Currey
ANTHONY POWELL:
                        Bernard Bergonzi
POWYS BROTHERS: R. C. Churchill
J. B. PRIESTLEY: Ivor Brown
PROSE WRITERS OF WORLD WAR I:
                        M. S. Greicus
HERBERT READ: Francis Berry
PETER SHAFFER: John Russell Taylor
BERNARD SHAW: A. C. Ward
EDITH SITWELL: John Lehmann
KENNETH SLESSOR: C. Semmler
C. P. SNOW: William Cooper
MURIEL SPARK: Patricia Stubbs
DAVID STOREY: John Russell Taylor
SYNGE & LADY GREGORY: E. Coxhead
DYLAN THOMAS: G. S. Fraser
G. M. TREVELYAN: J. H. Plumb
WAR POETS: 1914-18: E. Blunden
EVELYN WAUGH: Christopher Hollis
H. G. WELLS: Kenneth Young
ARNOLD WESKER: Glenda Leeming
PATRICK WHITE: R. F. Brissenden
ANGUS WILSON: K. W. Gransden
VIRGINIA WOOLF: B. Blackstone
W. B. YEATS: G. S. Fraser

EDWARD BOND: Simon Trussler
CHRISTOPHER ISHERWOOD:
                        Francis King
IRIS MURDOCH: A. S. Byatt

V. S. NAIPAUL: Michael Thorpe
P. H. NEWBY: G. S. Fraser
TOM STOPPARD: C. W. E. Bigsby
SWIFT: A. Norman Jeffares

Sir Walter Scott

Scott began his literary career as an editor of the traditional songs and ballads of Scotland and as a writer of romances in verse. In 1814 he published *Waverley*, the first of the series of books which established him as one of the most celebrated writers in Europe. Dr Jack examines Scott's merits as a novelist and his carelessness about the technique of his art; he emphasizes the degree to which Scott's imagination was visual; he traces Scott's part in revolutionizing the status of the novel, and in making mankind more aware than ever before of historical perspectives.

Dr Jack was born in Edinburgh, where his father was a Writer to the Signet and his great-grandfather had been one of Scott's successors as a Clerk of the Court of Session. A Fellow of Pembroke College, Cambridge, and University Lecturer in English, he is the author of *Augustan Satire*, of *English Literature 1815–1832* (the volume of the *Oxford History of English Literature* dealing with the period of Byron, Shelley and Keats), and of *Keats and the Mirror of Art*. He wrote the booklet on Pope which is No. 48 in this Series.

38pp. frontis. bibliog. 140 x 215mm paperback.

The Brontës

In this study in two volumes of the Series subtitled *The Formative Years* and *The Creative Work*, Winifred Gérin shows how in their first period the Brontës produced a collective juvenilia of astounding precocity in which, not only for reasons of age, Charlotte and Branwell were the leading spirits and prolific penmen. This was followed by a lyric period, corresponding to adolescence, of joint poetic output, in which Emily alone excelled, but in which Anne revealed genuine elegiac qualities, and Charlotte emerged as a writer of romantic novelettes already notable for their penetration into motive and character. Finally, after all of them had gained some experience of life, came the great period of novel-writing. . . .

Winifred Gérin is a Fellow and Council Member of the Royal Society of Literature, and has written full-length biographies on each of the four Brontës.

2 vols, plates, bibliog. 140 x 215mm paperback.

WRITERS & THEIR WORK

LONGMAN FOR THE BRITISH COUNCIL